T0160212

ALL MY FRIENDS ARE

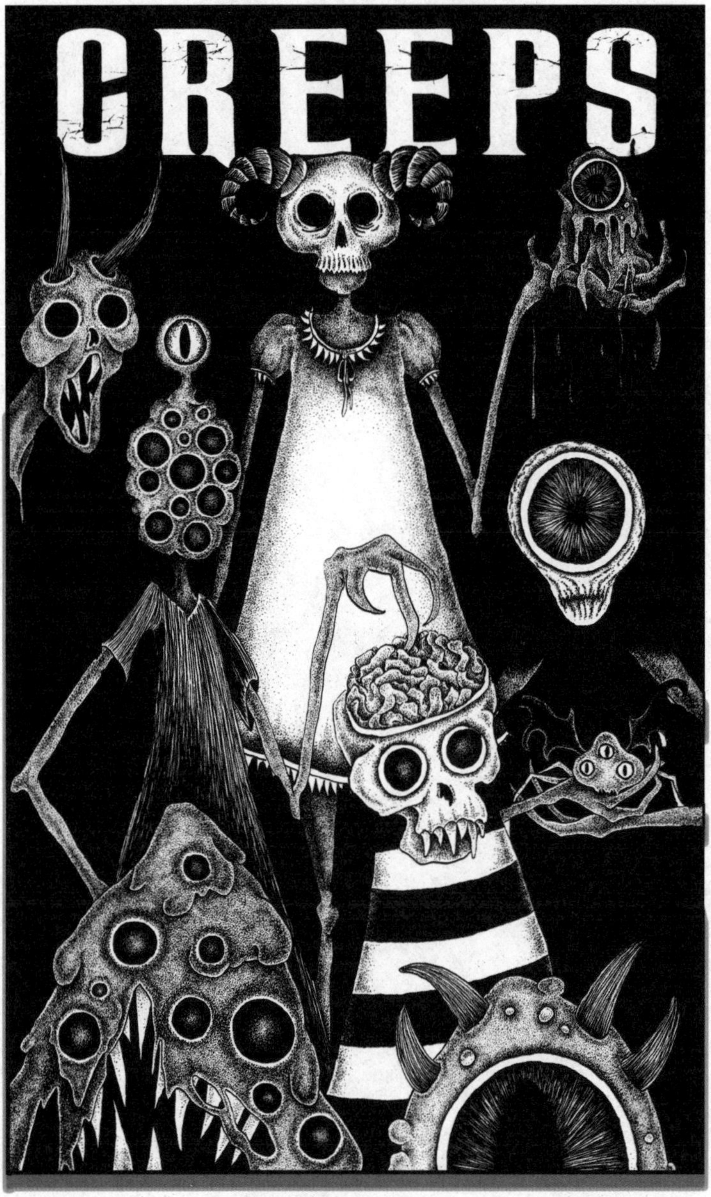
CREEPS

ALL MY FRIENDS ARE

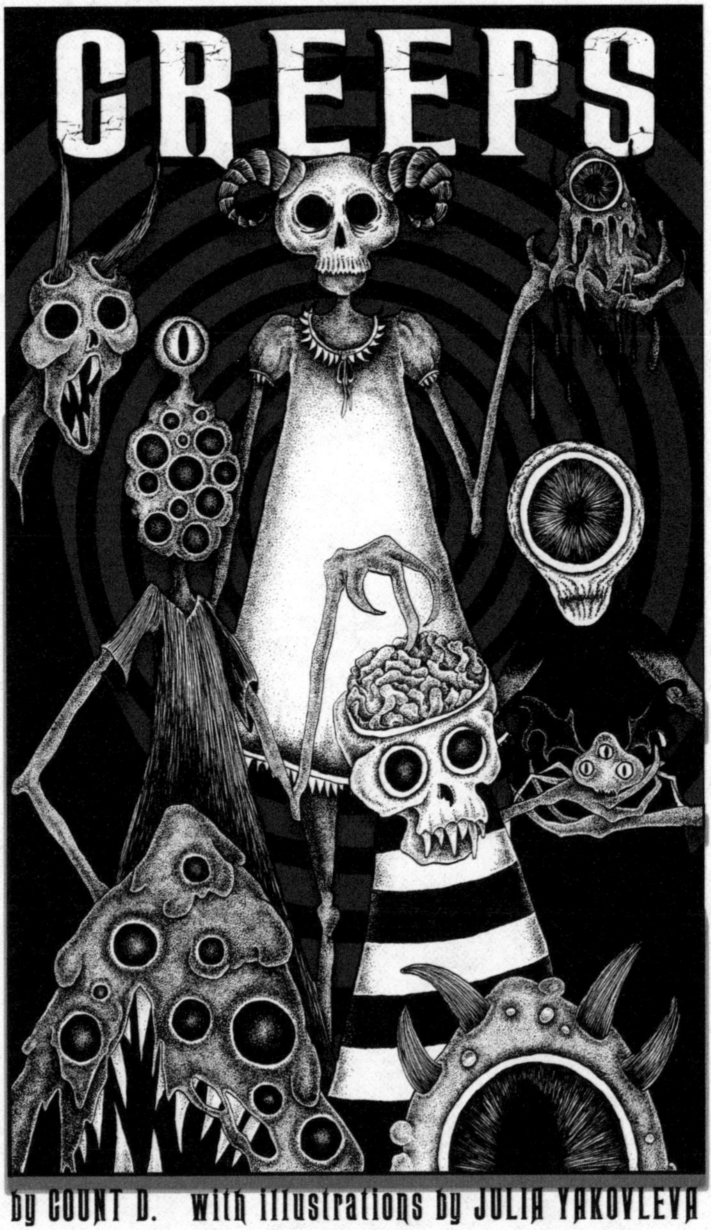
CREEPS

by COUNT D. with illustrations by JULIA YAKOVLEVA

RARE BIRD

Los Angeles, Calif.

THIS IS A GENUINE RARE BIRD BOOK

Rare Bird Books
453 South Spring Street, Suite 302
Los Angeles, CA 90013
rarebirdbooks.com

FIRST HARDCOVER EDITION

Set in Dante
Printed in the United States

10 9 8 7 6 5 4 3 2 1

Publisher's Cataloging-in-Publication Data
available on request.

I once had a dream that my dreams were not dreams,
and after it nothing was quite as it seemed.

CONTENTS

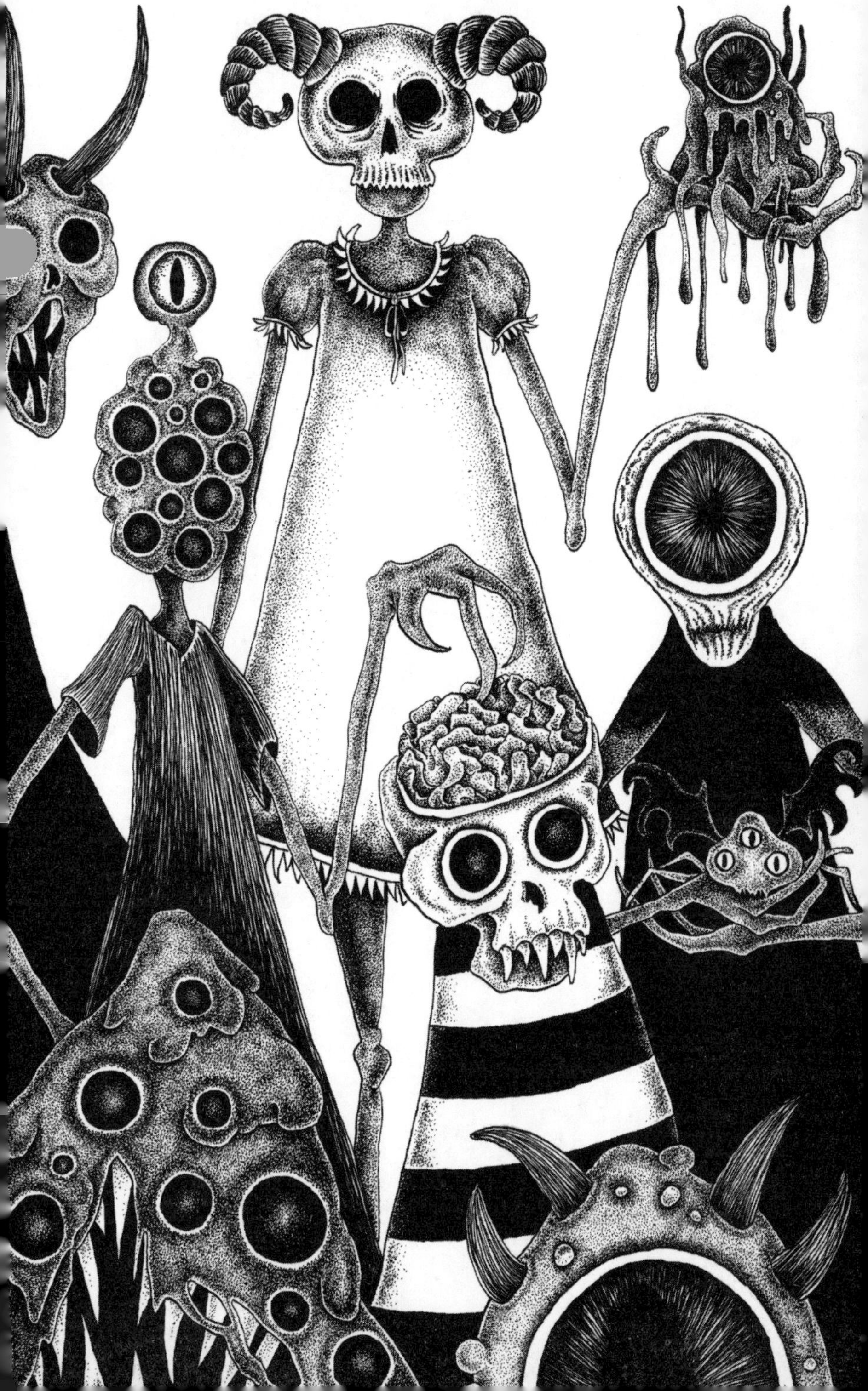

ALL MY FRIENDS ARE CREEPS!

We are the shadows where darkness crawls
And the spiderwebs between it all
We are the slither underneath your feet
All my friends are creeps!

We are the pain of the rotten tooth
Of every child with hallow loot
We are the snake in your kitten's tree
All my friends are creeps!

Some with horns and some with fangs
One hundred eyes, and giant brains
From the depths of the cosmic sea
All my friends are creeps!

We are blood drips on the knife
We are the coffin that fits just right
We are the grave with the vacancy
All my friends are creeps!

We are the fly in your baby food
Monsters of the foulest mood
We haunt every house and dream
All my friends are creeps!

We've come to take the night
These spirits never die
We're the eyes that you don't see
Beware!...All my friends are creeps!

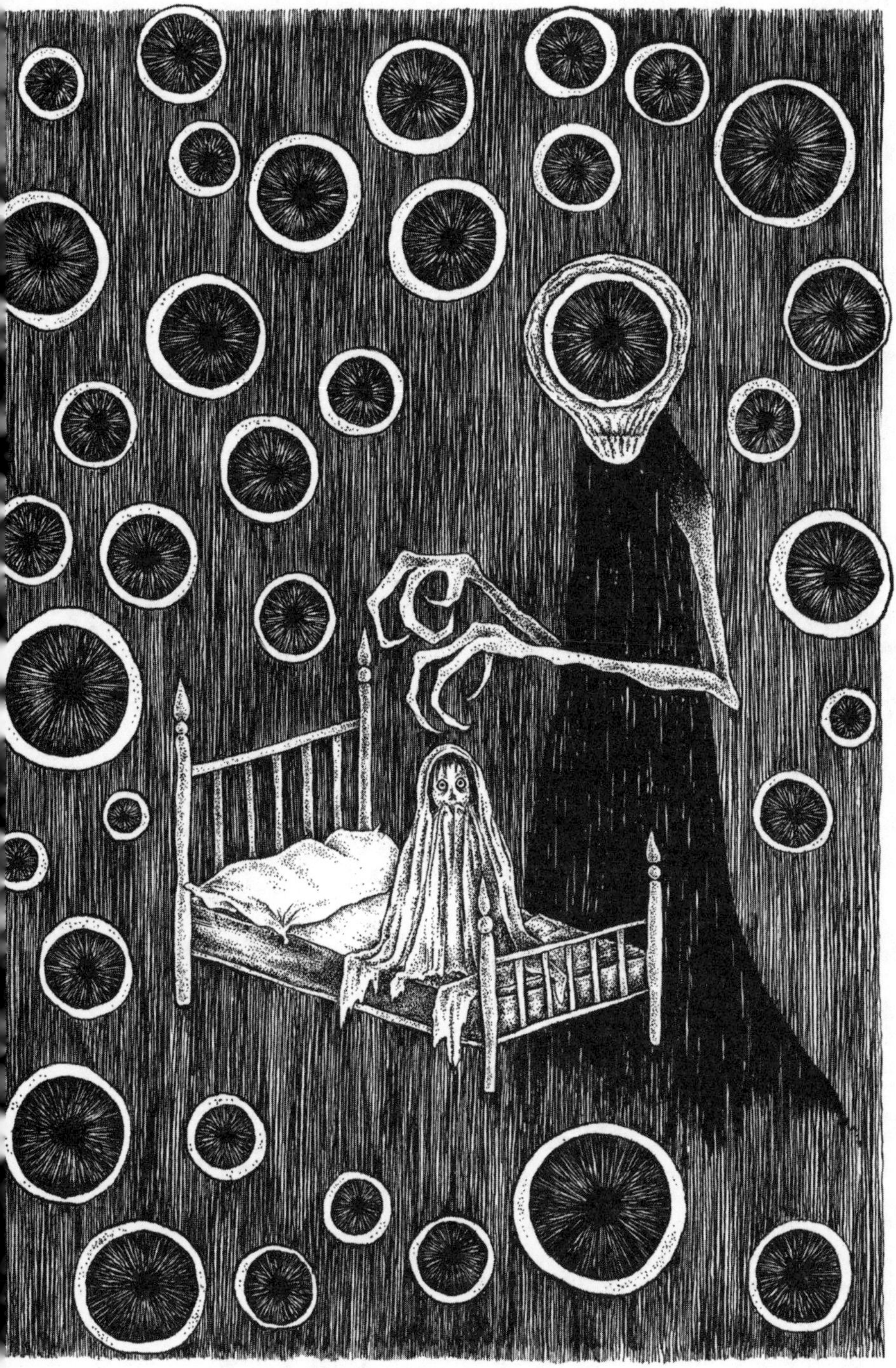

A ROOM FULL OF EYES

There is a room in this hall
and its walls are pitch black
not a window, nor an exit
in case of attack

You don't know when you're in it
but if you get out alive
you can say you've been seen
by one million eyes!

They've been there for years
and their focus is sharp!
They sit and they wait
for their show to start!

For every child that's lost
will wind up in this room
where someone's a witness
but no one knows whom!

They squint and they follow
and dart all around
no mouths and no noses
so they don't make a sound

Hide under your pillow,
and hold onto your bed!
Because this room full of eyes
is a room full of dread!

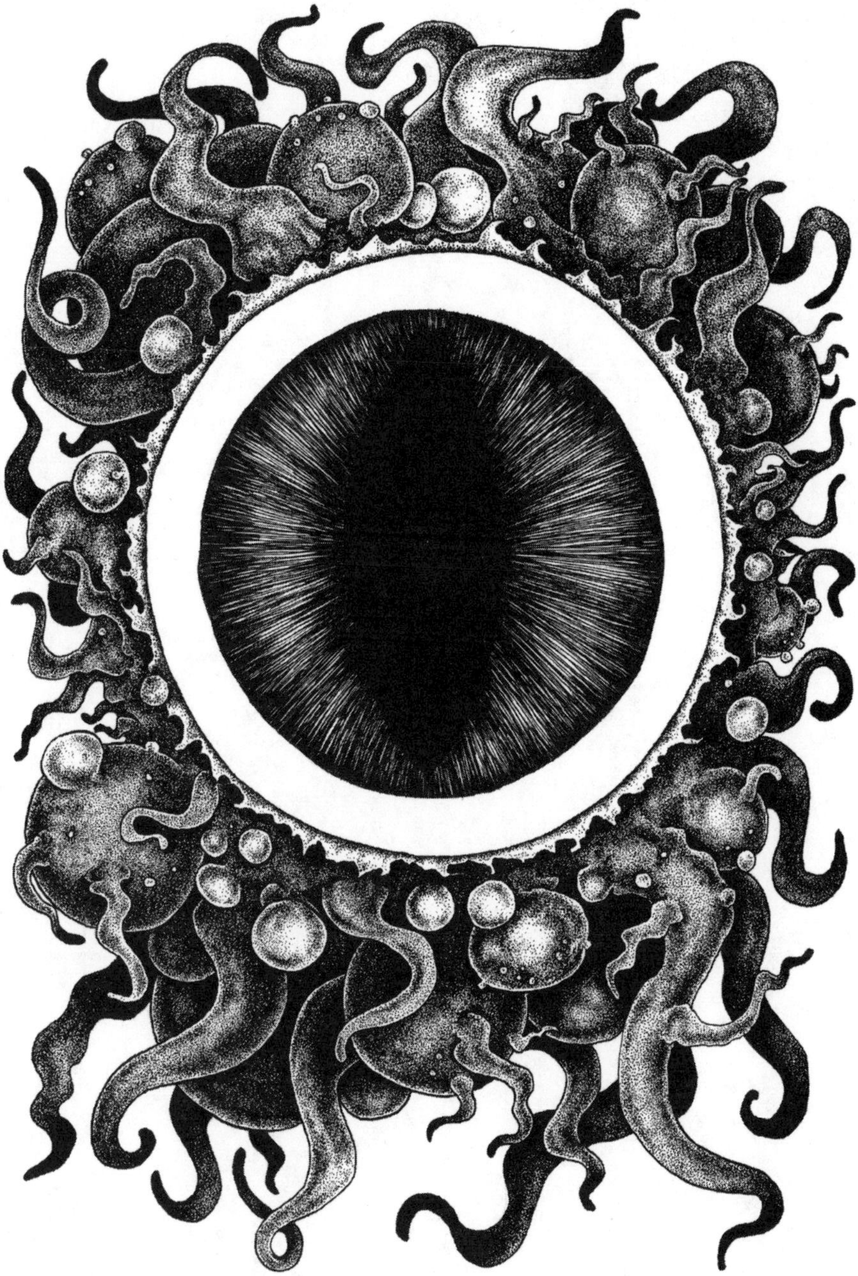

HERE COMES THE THING!

Here comes the thing
from a door deep in space
it doesn't have arms
or legs or a face!

The thing can see all
with its one giant EYE!
And it can hear whispers
and giggles and cries

It crawls around on its round,
green, blobbery butt
if you don't want it to find you,
best keep your door shut

It's from a place we can't see
because it's light-years away,
but this thing can find you
wherever you stay!

Beware of the thing
when you look to the moon
for the thing might look back
and then visit you soon!

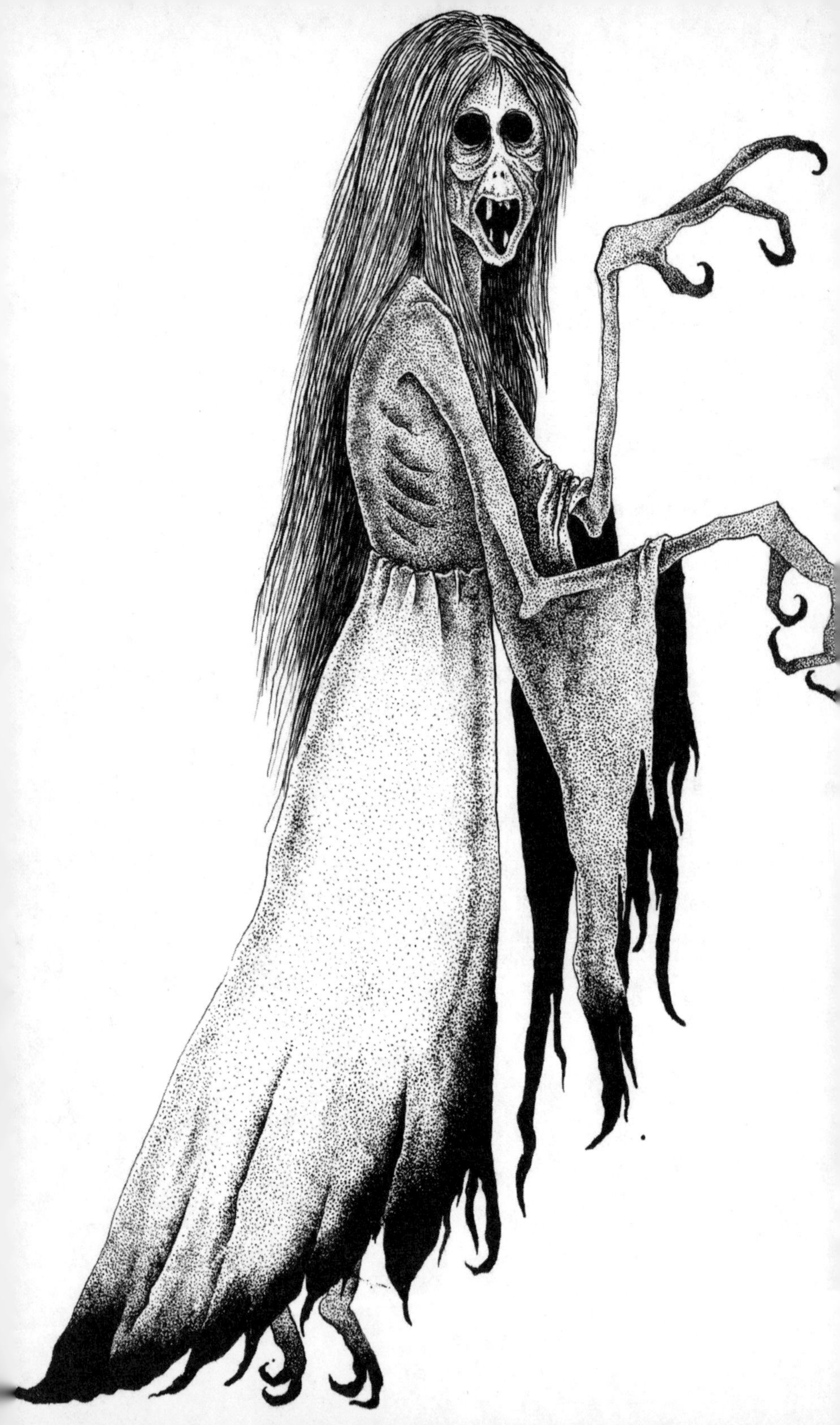

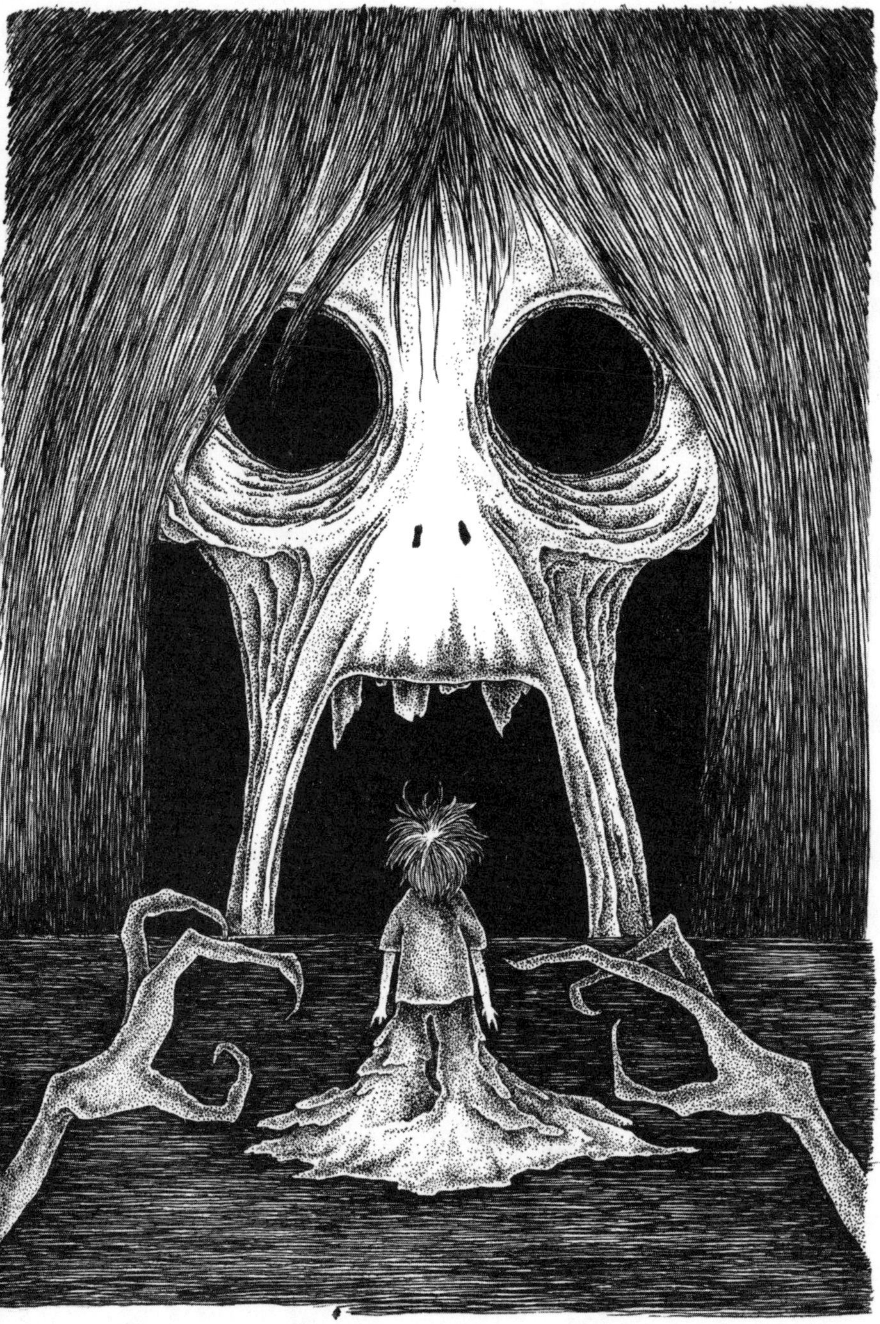

MUD ON MY SHOES

I dreamt of a woman
at the end of the hall
draped in blue light
and not moving at all.
She was sitting and waiting
for something to pass
just hissing so quiet
like a snake in the grass.
Her eyes were black marble,
all shiny and cold.
Her skin was so pale,
slimy and old.
The teeth she had left
were so rotten and green,
and as I tried to pass
her expression grew mean!
She opened her mouth
and let out a shriek!
But I could not run,
I had mud for feet!
Melting into the hallway
into a puddle of ooze,
the old woman laughed
and started to move!
Closer and closer,
as I sunk to the floor
she reached out her hands
and her fingers stretched more!
Hissing and spitting and pulling my hair!
I suddenly woke to find no one there!
Safe in my bed, and snug as bug
oh, but I went to school with shoes caked in mud!

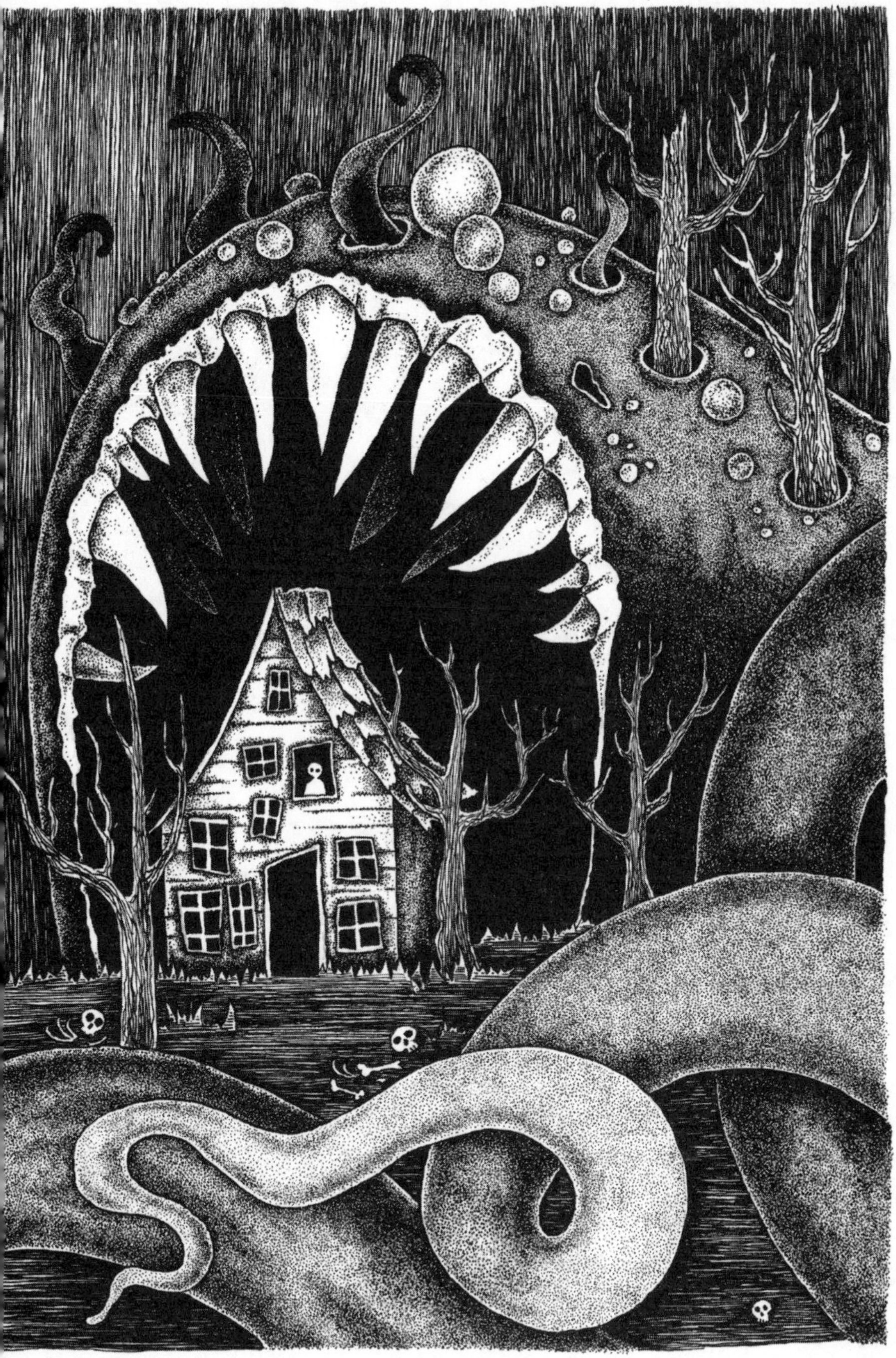

THE SLITHER THAT CAME FROM THE RIVER

There is a slither
that came from the river
the one on the edge of this town

it flows very slow
and at night has a glow
you can see it from miles around

on chill autumn nights
and with terrible fright
something slithers from the old blackened creek

it has not a conscious
it's as long as a train
with no hands, or eyes, or feet

just a mouth full of teeth
and it twists as it shrieks
as it slithers its way to your house

oh, there is a slither
that came from the river
and to IT you're the size of a mouse!

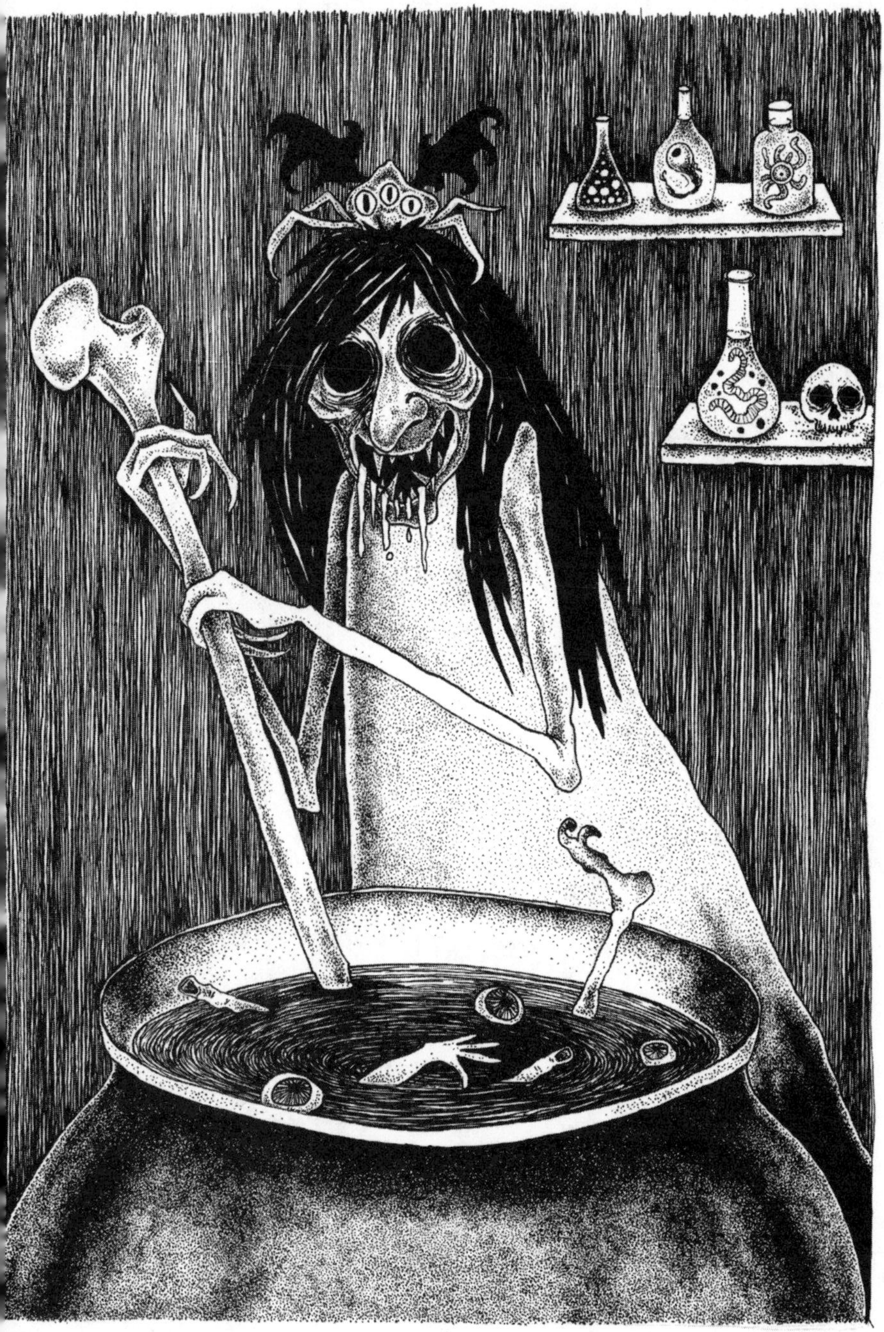

BEWARE OF THE WITCH!

Beware of the witch who lives in the woods
for she'd turn you into a bug if she could
she can jump out and grab you from any old tree
she's covered in filth and quite hard to see
she floats just above the wet, smooshy ground
but the witch only drools and makes not a sound
she's deciding if you're going to fly home or crawl
that is…if you make it much further at all

Beware of the witch who hides in your school!
Waiting and watching for some broken rule.
Near the principal's office, in a dark corridor
there's a little black room with a little black door.
Once you squish inside, you barely can breathe!
The witch will smell fear and sneak up to see
if you have all of your fingers and toes
she's just making a stew and wanted to know!

Beware of the witch who hides in your room!
Listen so close for the swoosh of her broom!
She waits until you will put down this book
and then flashlight your room for one final look
she knows the second that you fall asleep
and then out from your closet,
with her broom she will creep!
She'll come oh so close to your face on the bed
and wake you with one drip of drool on your head!

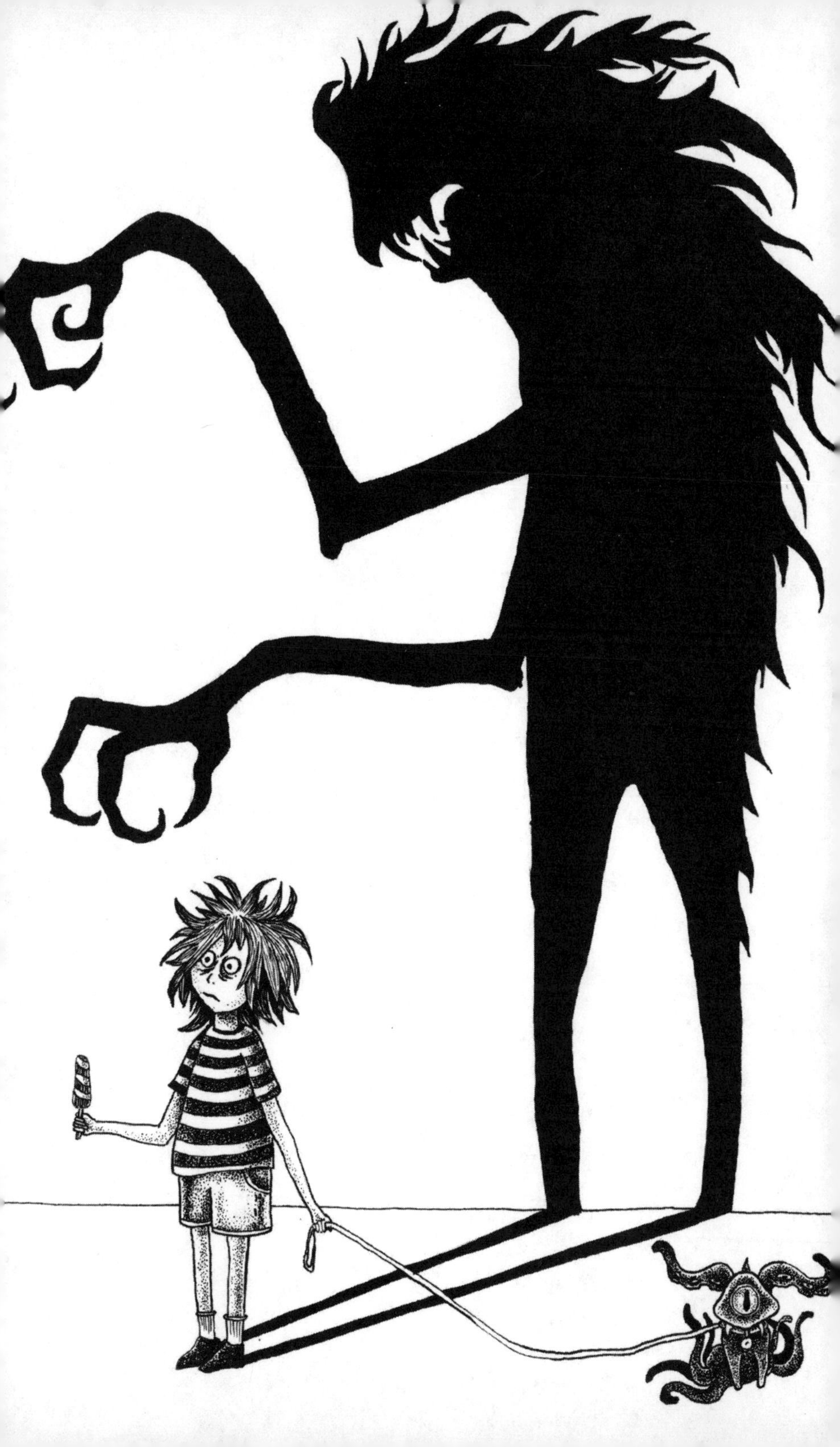

MY SHADOW

Wherever I go
my shadow goes!
It's behind my back
underneath my toes!
When I go to school
even when I go home
I'm never really fully alone.

When I go to bed
it rests on my head
on the very same pillow
on the very same bed!
If I'm very quiet
and don't make a peep,
just maybe one day
I'll be able to sleep.

Wherever I go
my shadows goes!
If I'm watching TV
or playing outside
I don't think there's anywhere left I can hide!
It watches me eat!
It watches me pee!
Can anyone tell it to just leave me be?

As long as I live
I'm never alone
because wherever I go…
my shadow will know!

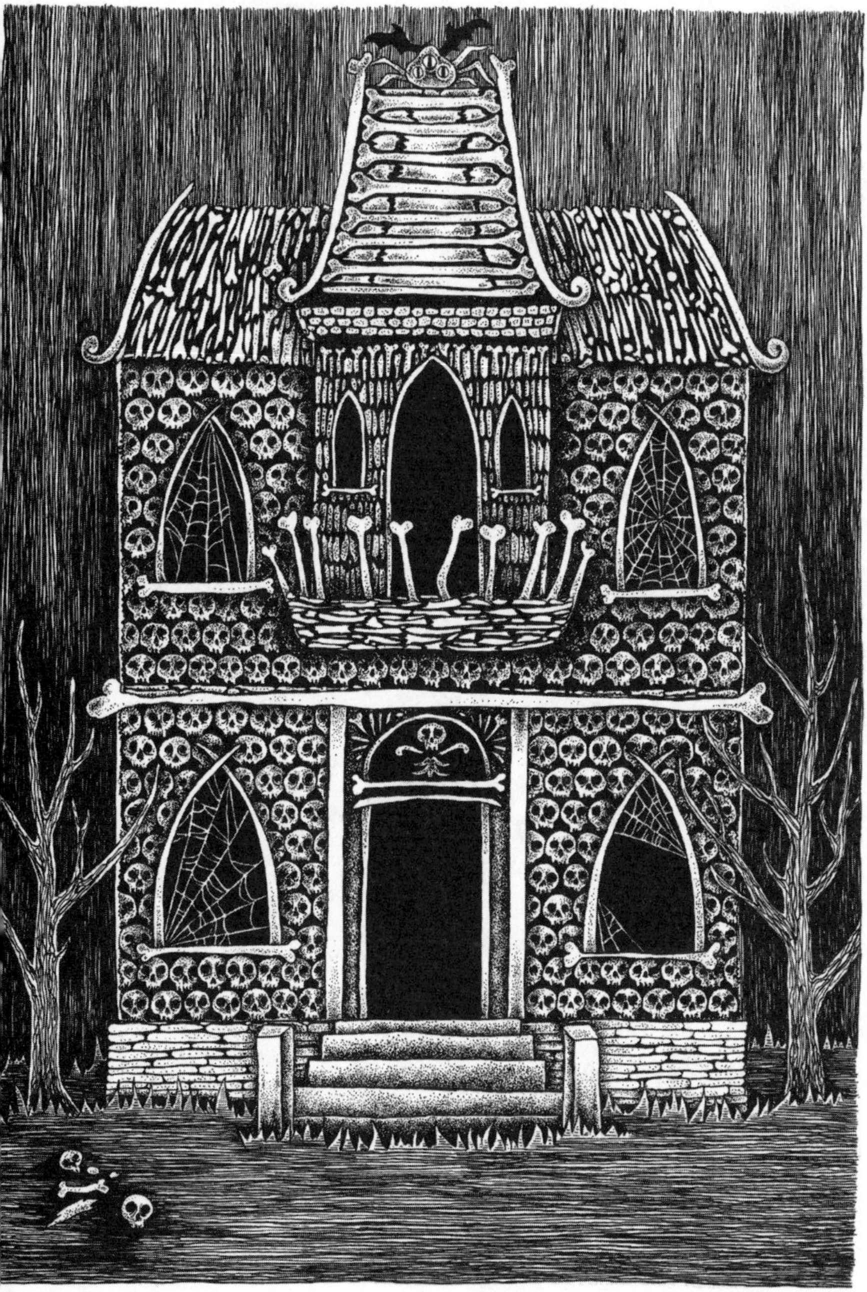

THE HOUSE OF ANGRY BONES

A hundred years past
and miles away
were some people whose land
was taken away

Their loss was a horror
of bloodshed and tears
but in their memory, a house
stood erected for years

Every inch of its frame
was constructed from bone
from every life lost
its very nails sewn

The house had a feeling
and a will of its own
turning bitter and angry
from a once quiet home

Cursing and plaguing
every soul through its door
and for every soul captured
it expands one room more!

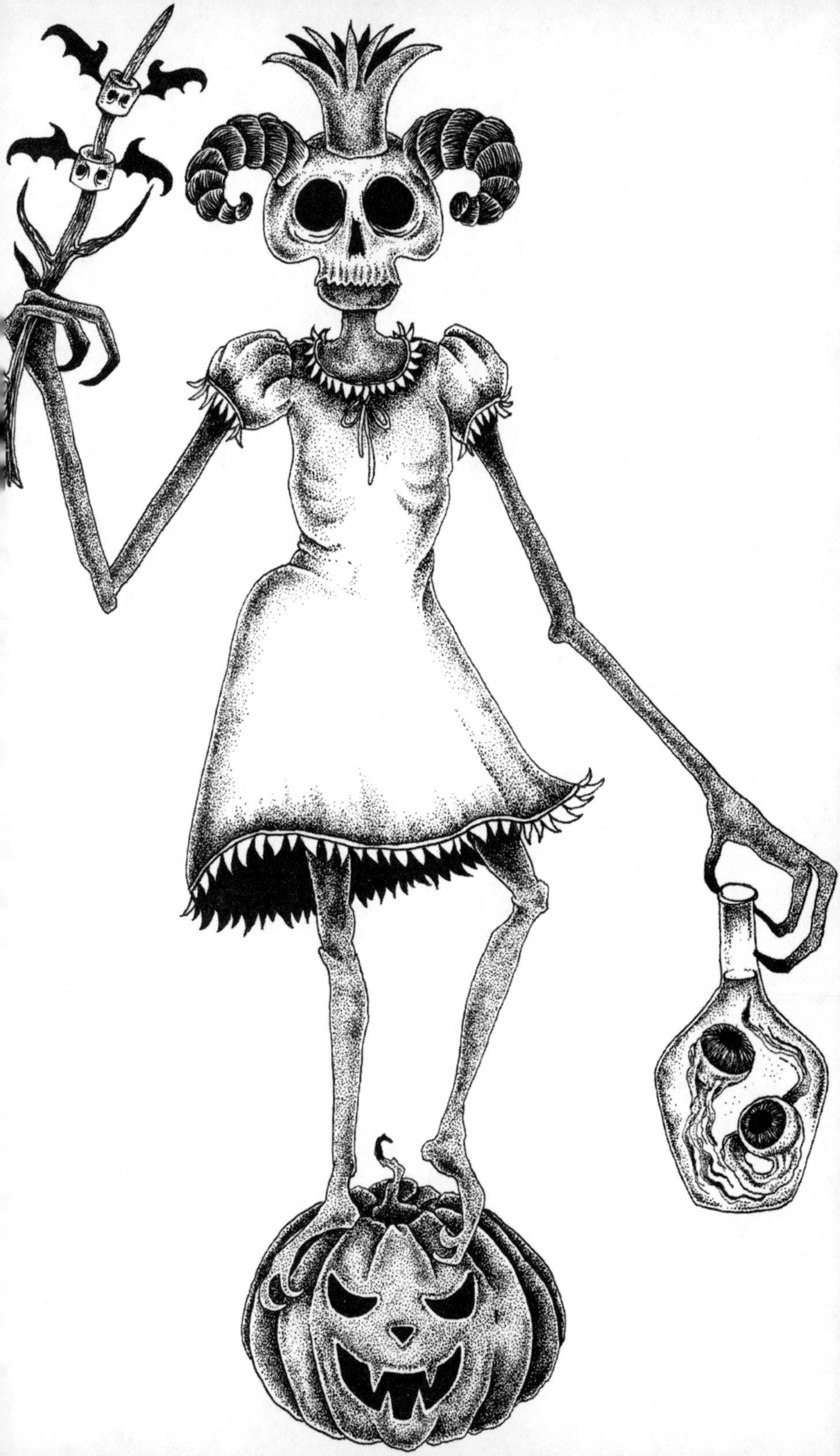

HALLOWEEN

Halloween, Halloween

yay for me, it's Halloween!
I love the orange and black and yellow
the candy corns and bat marshmallows
Halloween is just for me!
I'll be anything I want to be!
I can be a robot or a clown
a hero who can save this town
I can be a monster or a queen
an astronaut or anything!
Halloween, oh Halloween
I'll tell you what you mean to me
a time to laugh and boo with glee
a time to spook and trick or treat
Halloween, Halloween
yay for me, it's Halloween!

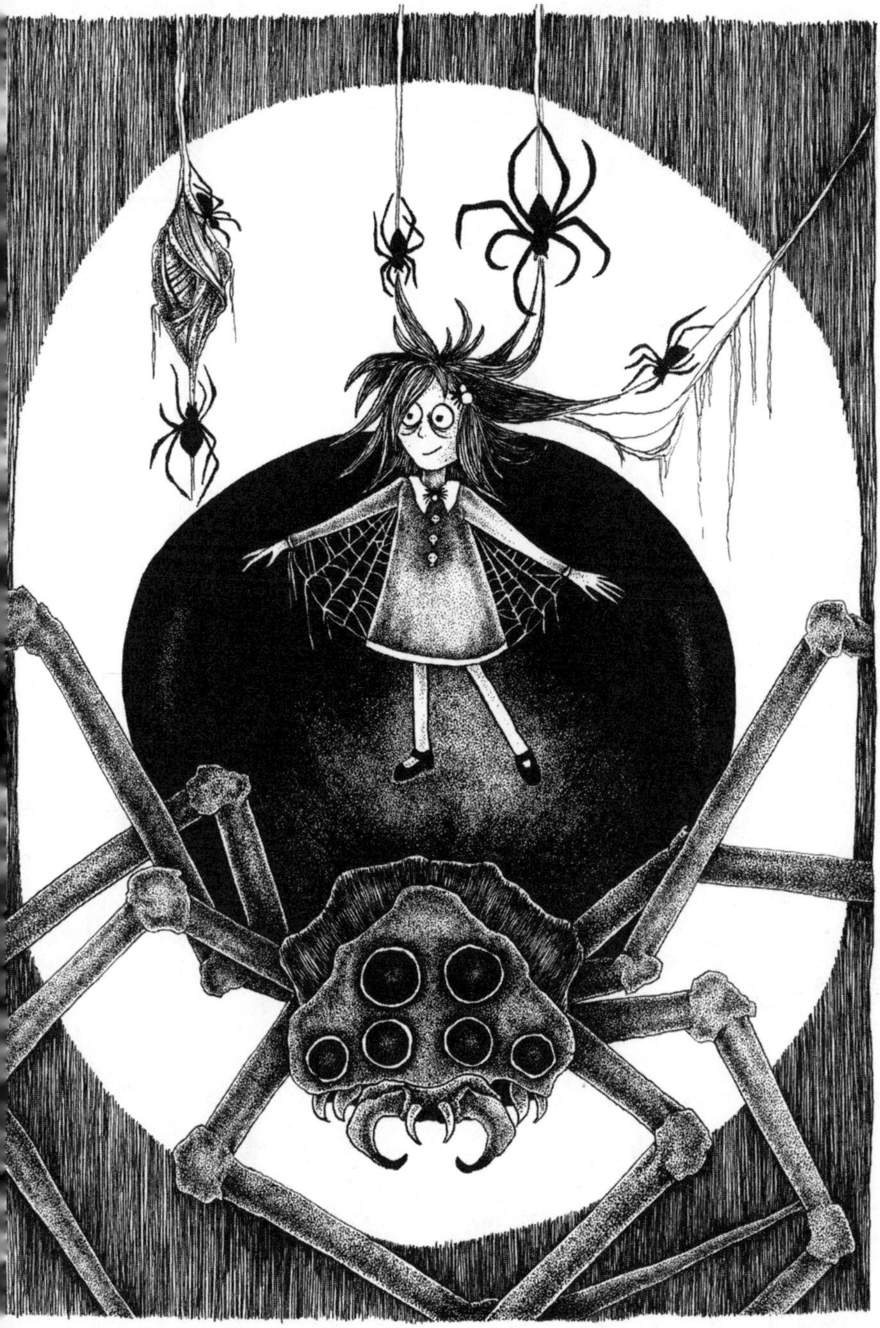

MOLLY MACABRE

Molly Macabre once climbed down a well
and came back with many a story to tell
a whole kingdom of spiders that bowed at her feet
she had clothes made of silk and all the flies she could eat

The spiders were grateful for such nice a guest
They made her feel at home in their underground nest
Her hair would be combed by millions of hands
while Molly spoke of adventures and exotic new lands

She seemed like a princess in this place she came from
now with a kingdom of creatures never feeling the sun
for underneath is a world much different than ours
much colder and darker, with endless black hours

Then suddenly Molly's name, called from above
her dinner was ready, and she needed a shove
"Hurry…! Please hurry, before she calls again!
Can I call on the help of my eight-legged friends?"

"Please carry me high to the top of the well
and I promise to come back with good news to tell!"
They locked all their arms and with furious might
Molly flew up the well, toward the fading sun light

And just as her mother came calling again
she saw Molly ascend from hole where she hid
but before Mom could ask how she got underground
she fainted and fell with a horrible sound!

Molly was covered in some frightening pests
"Hello, Mother, I brought home a few dinner guests!"

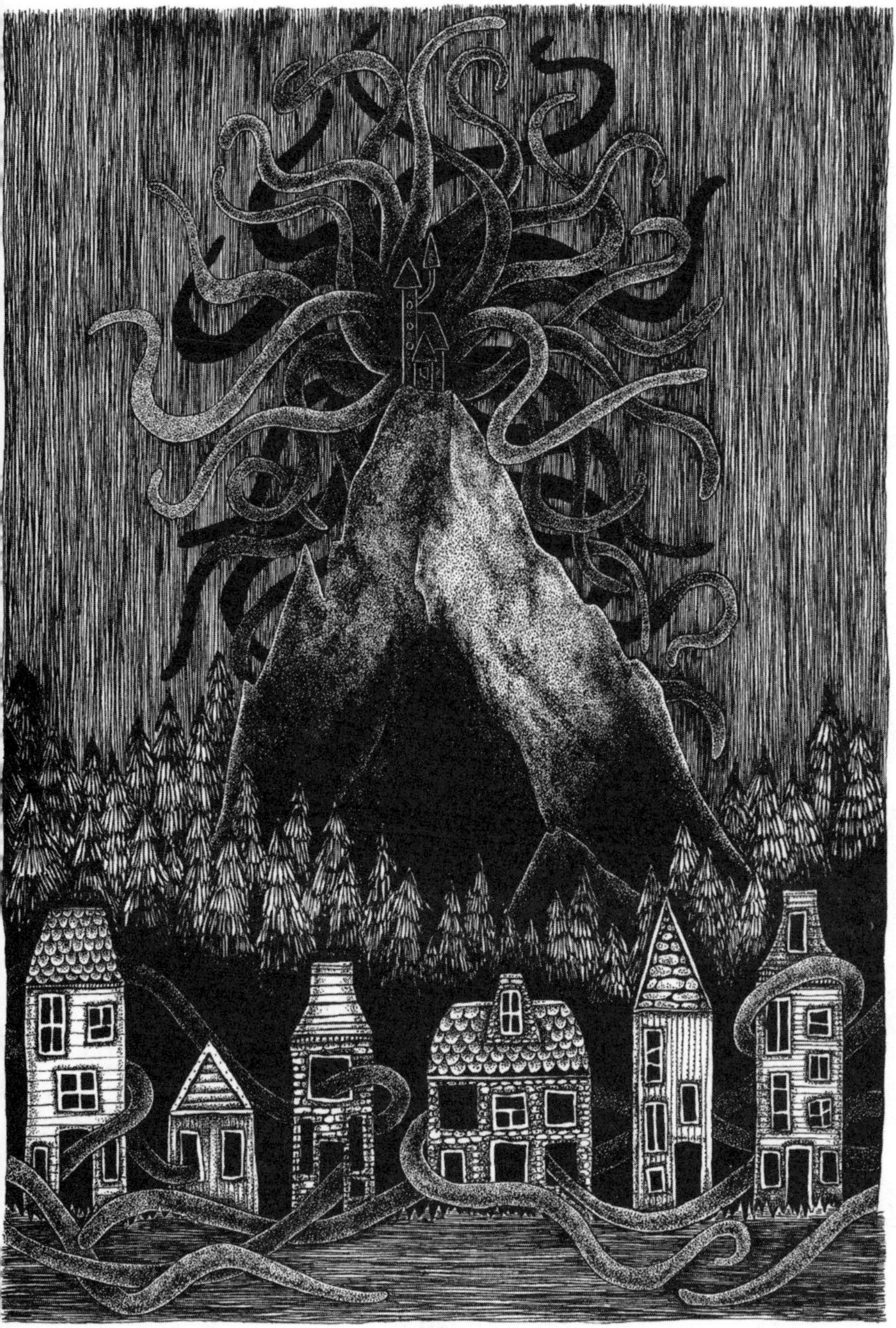

AT THE TOP OF DOOM MOUNTAIN

At the top of Doom Mountain
is a crooked black house
and sits inside is an old
wicked housekeeper, Klaus

his job is to guard
the door to beneath
where all the doom of Doom Mountain
does quietly sleep

one day it will rise,
and then so will Klaus,
to open the gate
and step out of his house

so the doom can escape
on any limb, wing, or spell
the skies turned to black,
and the last rainbow fell

Doom blocks the sun,
turning days into nights,
then tapping on windows,
and doors to a fright!

Doom finds a way in,
through every crack in the floor
through every pipe, lock, and dream,
and then comes back for more!

in any size, shape, or name
the Doom can appear
casting shadows on all,
like a blanket of fear

Klaus lights a light
and sits in a chair
watching skies for the smoke
to soon fill the air

the Doom will return
for another long sleep
to the crooked black house
with its housekeeper Creep!

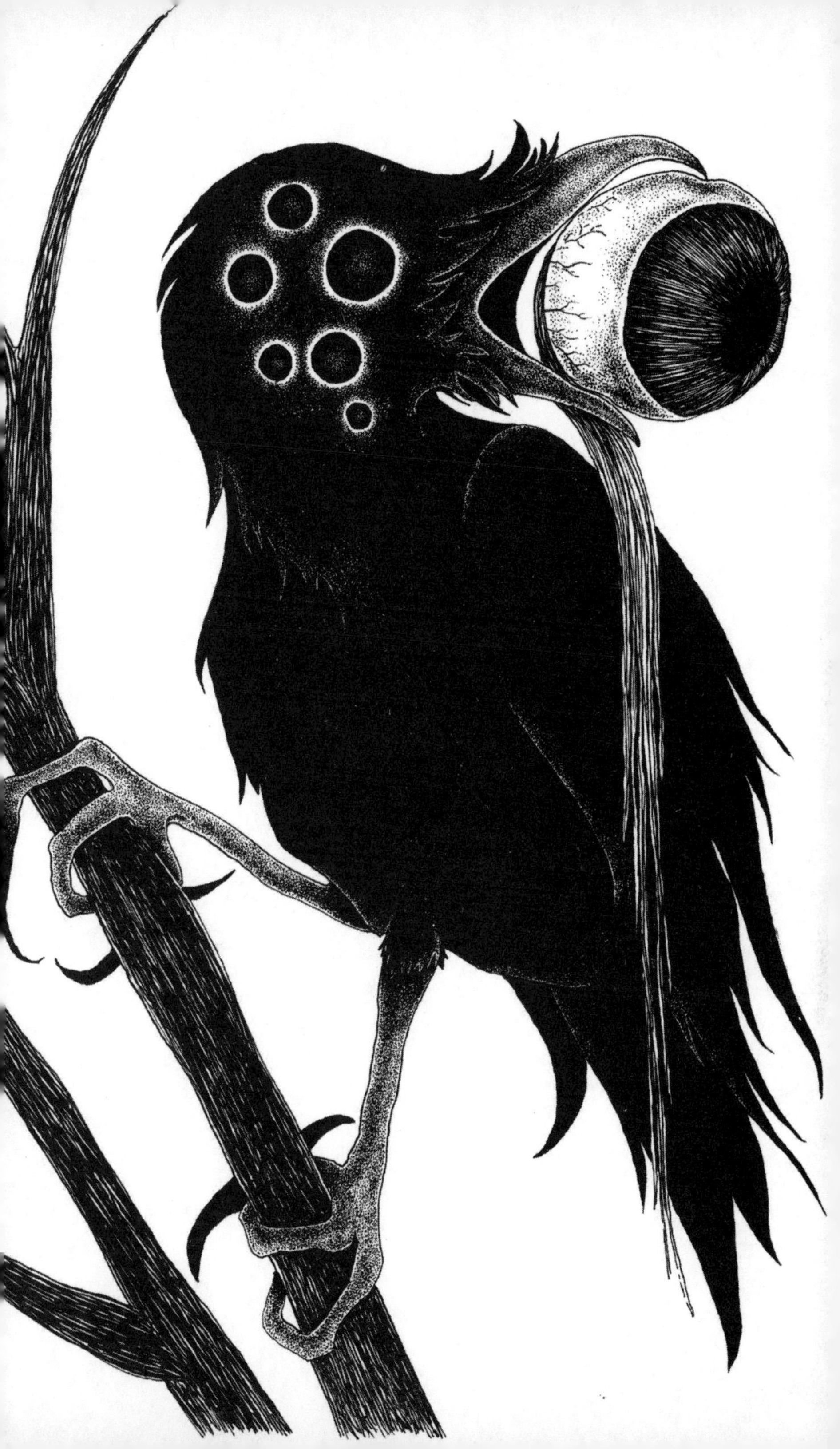

BLACKBIRD BLUES

Monday morning came on a wing
blacker than soot, and faster and mean
warning of a truth that's just up and died
saying there's a storm coming, you best run and hide
it will free you from all the pain that you knew
when you hide under wings of the old blackbird blues

A foot stomp and clap will scare them away
while we hustle and bustle through each dreaded day
warning of fire that burns like the sun
no heart is extinguished until damage is done
it will cure all that ails you, and other stuff too
when you sing along to the old blackbird blues

She wore diamonds for eyes, and they shined like the sea
smiles in the sun with genuine glee
now a picture of consequence, for those in the know
there is no safety from the lottery crow
for the beast took her eyes, and all her demons too
when she shook to the sound of the old blackbird blues!

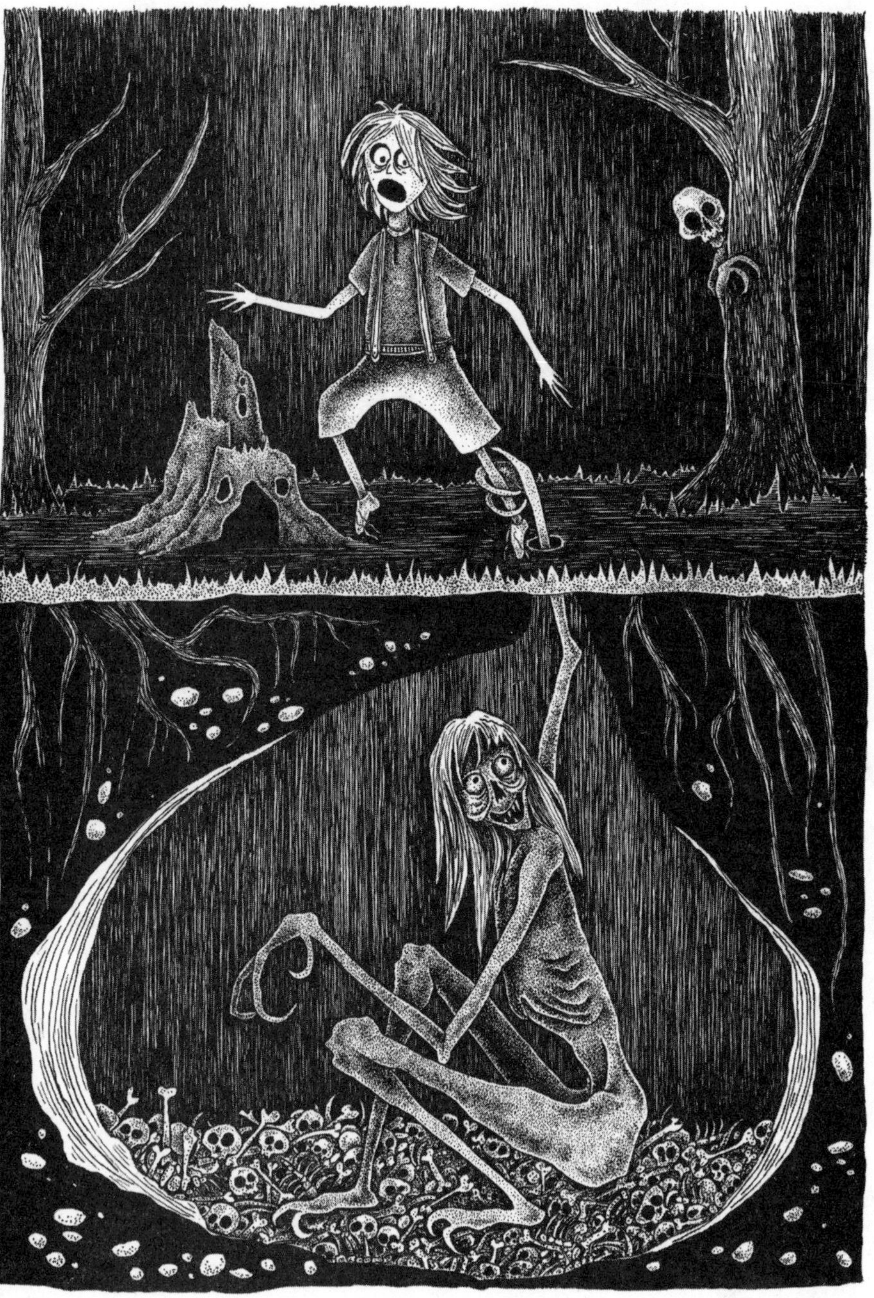

THE TOWN THAT WITHERED

The old dark house at the end of the road
is a very strange place where nobody goes.
It creaks in the night, as the wind moves its bones.
There's a tapping and rapping, as if somebody's home.

But the old dark house has been empty for years,
there once lived a widow who had drowned in her tears.
For her husband went missing on All Hallows' Eve,
on a leisurely walk through the New England leaves.

Some blamed a beast who lived in the brush.
Others cried murder from anonymous crush.
One said a serpent had come down from the sky
and carried poor Mr. Withers deep into the night

His body had vanished, and his tracks blown away,
as if swallowed whole by the dark in some way.
His widow would search every corner and creek,
but not a hair was found of her beloved Pete.

He was a cheerful old boy who everyone loved!
And he once ran for mayor with his wife's loving shove.
"I'll fix the roads! And I'll build a new school!
I know just the spot, so bring all of your tools!"

The whole town went to work on Peter's new plan!
The kids were so happy to have a playground with sand!
Now recess had swings and slides up and down,
and a new field for sports in the middle of town.

As if sleeping for years, the town came alive!
Booming and bustling, the economy thrived!
All the townspeople smiled at Pete on his walks,
"Good day, Mr. Withers!"…always stopping to talk.

Then one autumn day, some small shoes were found.
Alone, without feet, on the shiny playground.
An unfinished sandcastle, shovel to the side,
where young Billy was playing, now nowhere to find.

A few days of terror then covered the town!
Everyone pointing fingers at old ladies and clowns!
But then two more went missing.
Just shoes left in sand,
with no sign of struggle or foul play at hand.

A darkness had fallen, and the town didn't sleep!
With each week that passed, another child they'd seek!
With the shoes piling up and the mystery so thick,
the town became angry...and chased Pete with sticks!

"Everything was just fine! Until you came along!
Let's build this and that!...What could go wrong?"
The town didn't know that the new schoolhouse bell
had been waking the dead from some old ancient spell!

For the swing set was built on a graveyard so deep.
Massive caverns of bones, where the angry dead sleep.
For hundreds of years, they had sat undisturbed,
rotting and waiting for their cries to be heard!

One by one, children lost into the blackest of nights.
Till every soul of the town would vanish from sight.
The young ones went first, then the husbands, then wives.
Even pets disappeared, and the rivers went dry.

Mrs. Withers was last, living decades alone.
All black every day, her face never shown.
She never left that house at the end of the road
in the old town called Withers, where nobody goes!

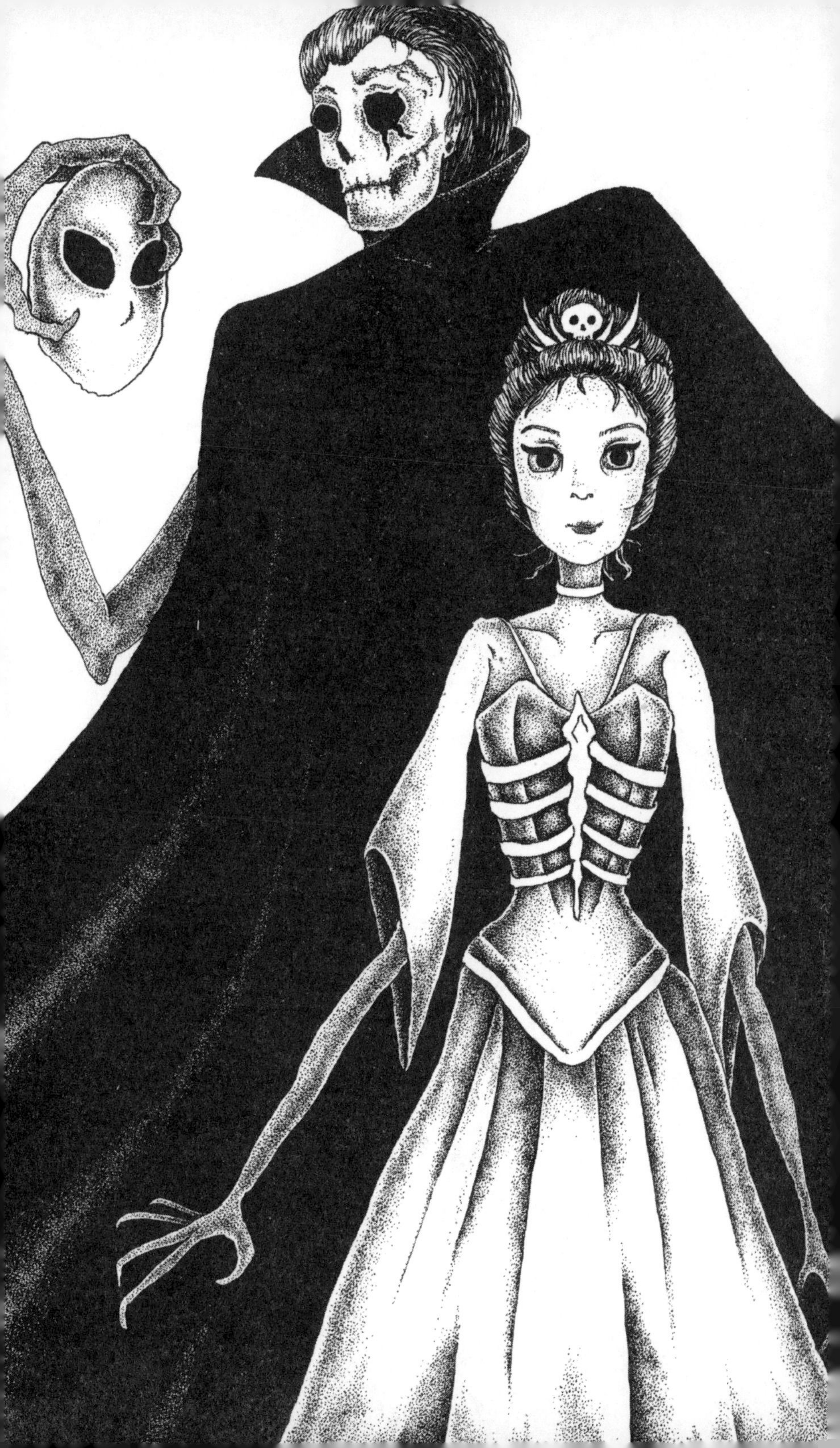

CHRISTINE

Eric sat alone on his organ bench
playing his sorrows away.
For Christine would never love a man
who ever looked this way.
So he thought, "I'll wear a mask
and hide my shocking face!
I'll wait in the shadows till she's alone
and charm her with my grace!"
Eric sat tight, waiting for night
to fall on their old opera house.
He played a new song so sweetly,
he hypnotized every bug and mouse!

Her hair was tied neat upon her head
as she stepped from her formal gown.
All alone in her mind and corset
came a strange and haunting sound.
She began to sing like an angel choir,
that could fill the heavens wide.
She had longed to meet a music man,
to play right by her side.
Together they filled the night with sound
created from thin air.
And Christine began to follow the tune,
not stopping until there!

In a darkened cave with candles lit,
Eric played unmasked, out loud!
Thinking, "This is closest that I'll ever be
to ever feeling proud!"

Christine approached behind him,
harmony in perfect blend…
"If I turn around, our music will stop,
and we'll never sing again!"

"No!…Sing," she said,
"and play all the notes
that fly like birds of heart.
Play the melodies that soar
and comfort us in dark…
Play me anything you hear,
or anything that's true!
Play your soul for all to see,
that's all I ask of you!"

Eric smiled for the first time
and then slowly turned around.
She didn't run or gasp in fear,
she didn't even make a sound!
She smiled back and touched his face
with her soft and loving hand.
"I've searched my whole life
for a song to sing,
and I've found it in this man."

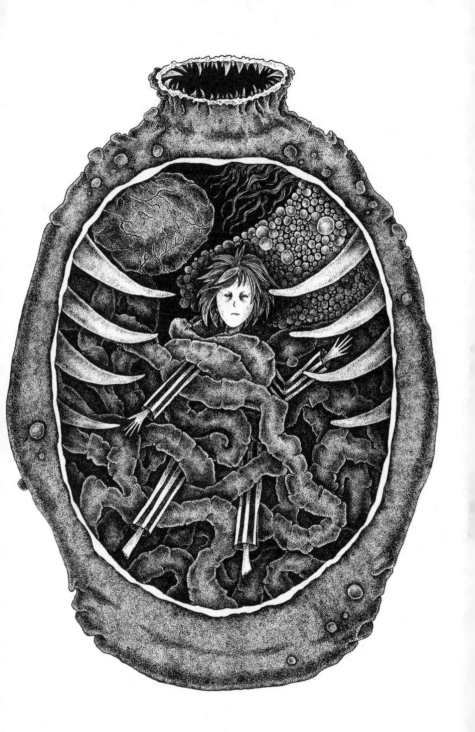

IN THE BELLY OF THE BEAST

When Stan poked his belly,
it seemed to be jelly,
but a kind that was soft and warm.
He found a hole in the middle,
where his finger would fiddle
and burrow like a hungry worm.

"What is it I'll find?"
said young Stan in his mind.
"Maybe there's money I forgot to spend?
Or perhaps some candy!
Wouldn't that be dandy?
But I don't want to share with my friends!"

So he waited till home,
and when he was alone,
he got a flashlight from under his bed.
He said goodnight to his mother
and dived under covers,
making a tent with his head.

He plotted and schemed,
and with a devious gleam,
he drew up a blueprint and plan.
His army men would stand by
and his fingers would pry.
"If I could only just slip in my hand!"

But once he got a fist in,
then he could do it again,
"Maybe a foot with a twist and a shout?"
When the last toe was gone,
hen it wasn't too long,
until his head was the last to stick out!

Stan looked like a creature
from a midnight feature
when his flashlight rolled *bang* to the floor!
Then down the hall came Mother
and a scurry of covers,
until her shadow eclipsed the door…

Then in a panic,
and Stan feeling quite manic,
closed his eyes and gritted his teeth.
Then he wiggled his head,
"I'll hide inside instead,
there's no way she'll ever catch me!"

As the door opened wide
with a gasp and the light
from the hallway that shined on the bed…
Stan disappeared
and with his mother in tears…
Stan's belly had eaten his head!

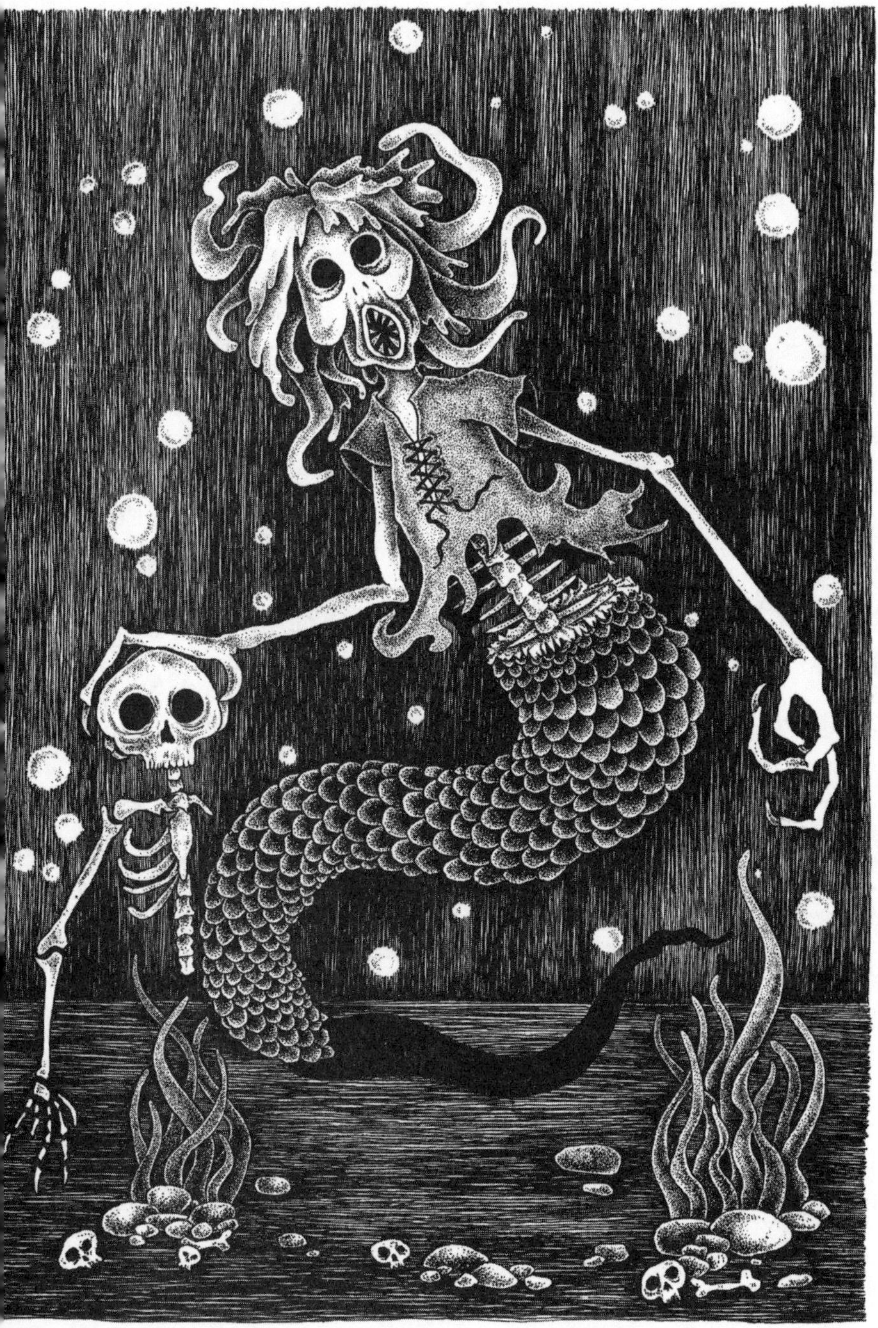

THE SEA WITCH

She's the salt of the air
and the chill in the breeze
she's the force of the tide
the shells in your feet
her hair is a slimy
and strangling green
that pulls you into
the blackening deep.
with the palest of skin
never kissed by the sun,
she's a hypnotic siren
that no minnow outruns!
she wails through the night
with a hollow shell sound
every sea horse will swim
from miles around
as she lures the ships
to crash into rocks!
and swallows the children
that play on the docks!
nails like the teeth
of the greatest white shark
and with an octopus grip
she'll rip you apart!
commanding all crabs
and lobsters to pinch!
for no creature is safe
from the dreaded sea witch!

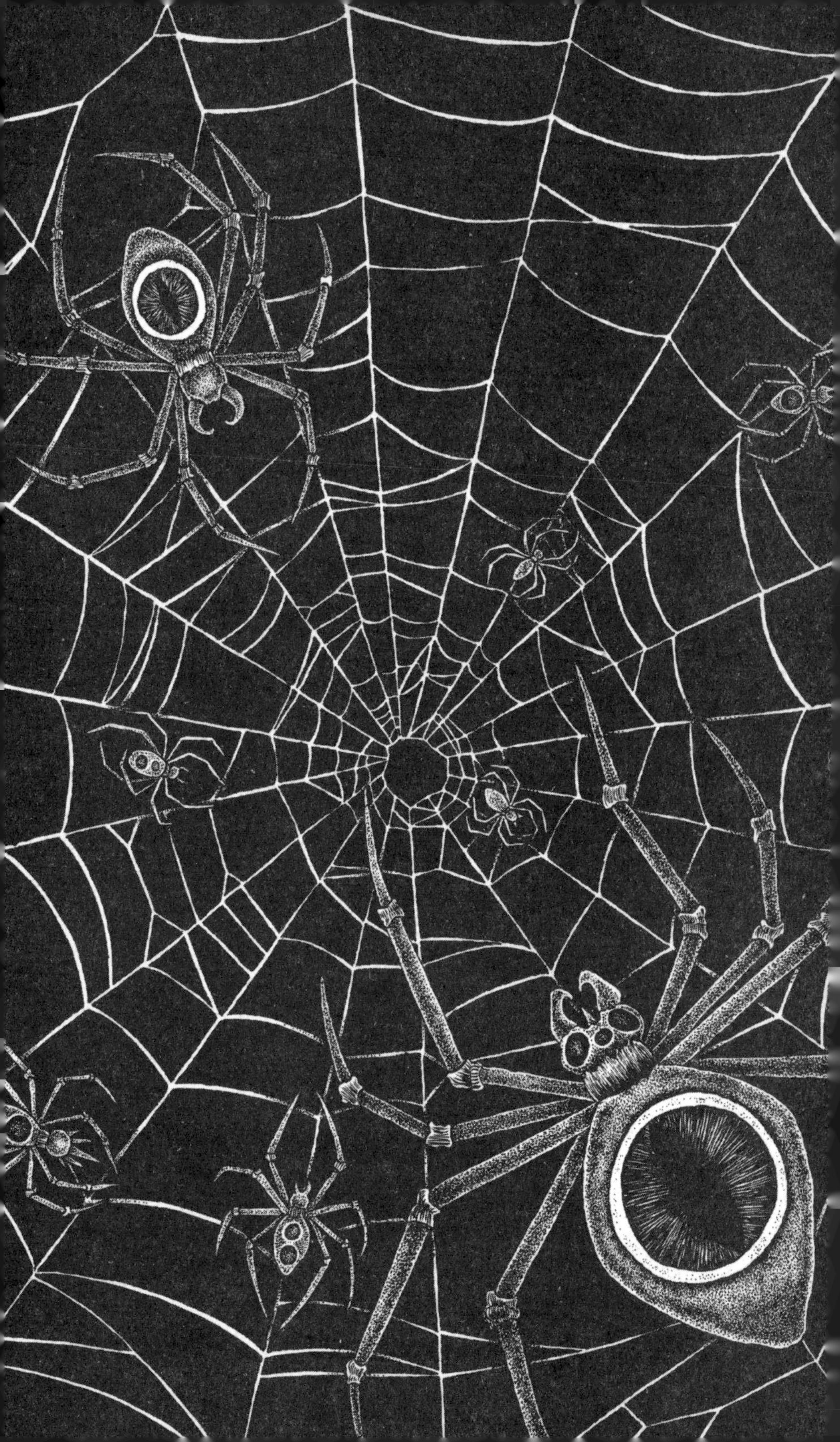

SPIDERWEBS IN SUNSHINE

On afternoons on this old porch
in the lattice-covered vines
is a house of spiders full of webs
with busy, busy lives

I see them come outside and sit
on their roof in fading sun
warming each and every leg
and stretching one by one

They go back inside and settle down
for a savory entrapped feast
of fly that landed in the webs
that laid down for defeat

Tomorrow one might journey out
on front-yard errands close
gathering all supplies they need
to be such gracious hosts

Spider webs in sunshine
daylight monsters all so real
plotting, scheming, eating, and screaming
murder every meal!

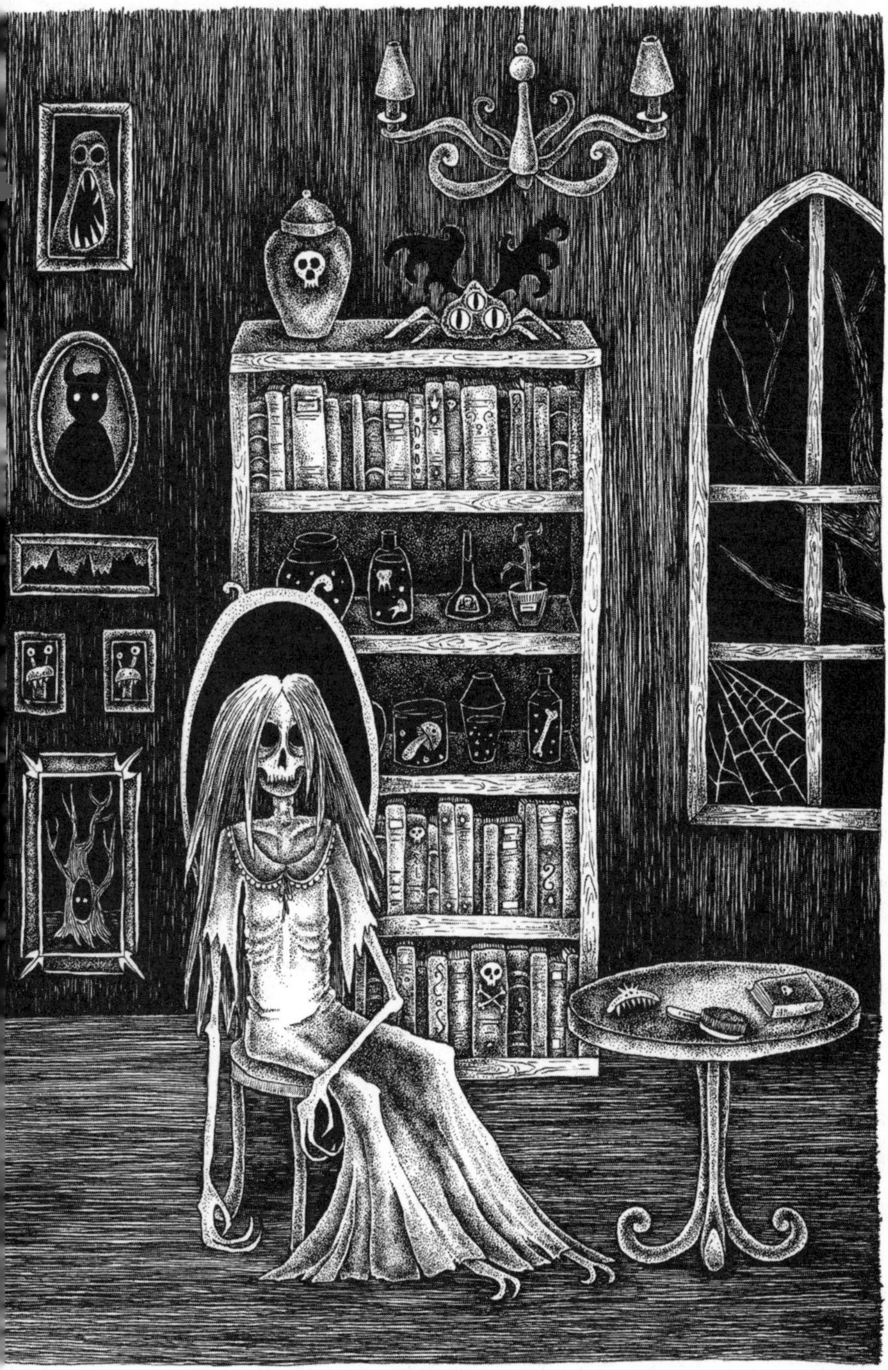

REBECCA EVILLE

Rebecca Eville lived up on a hill,
far from anyone or anything.
She hated the sun, and she hated fun,
and pretty rainbows, and birds that sing.

She hated the sky, but didn't even know why.
Perhaps it was too high to reach?
She even hated the ground, and would stomp with a sound,
and pout if she went to the beach!

"I won't leave my house…and just scurry about!
Meeting this person and talking about that!
I don't need a thing!…Not a child, nor ring!
And I've got no time for a dog or a cat!"

So from winter through fall, no one called at all,
and at Christmas not a card was sent.
She sat all alone in her big empty home,
with every penny that she never spent.

Then ten became twenty…even fifty, not plenty
years alone for Rebecca Eville…
Who died in her chair, having just combed her hair
for no one, she now sits very still.

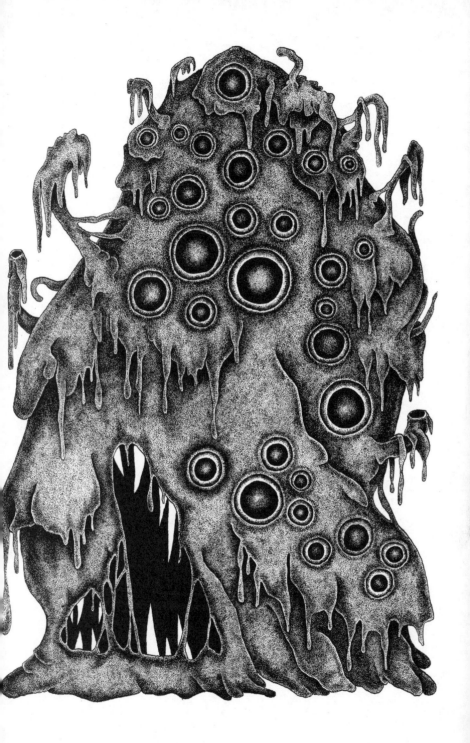

THE SPOOKEDY, GOOPEDY,
SLIPPERY, SCHLOPP

From the depth of the oceans came a gelatinous wave
that covered the shore with thick slimy haze
a blob of a beast weighing ten thousand tons
every creature in sight would tremble and run
a strangling ooze of any color or size
and loaded with millions of tiny black eyes

Drippity, glippity, slippity, klop
slides the horrible body of the Spookedy Schlopp!

The children all came from miles around
when Spookedy oozed from the toxified ground
bubbling and gurgling and howling so loud
then flopping and plopping through the terrified crowd
Spookedy stretched over buildings so high
swallowing hundreds of thousands of lives

Beware of the slow, deep, slithering sound
it might mean a slow, deep death is abound
drippity, glippity, goopedy, glop
slides the horrible body of the Spookedy Schlopp!

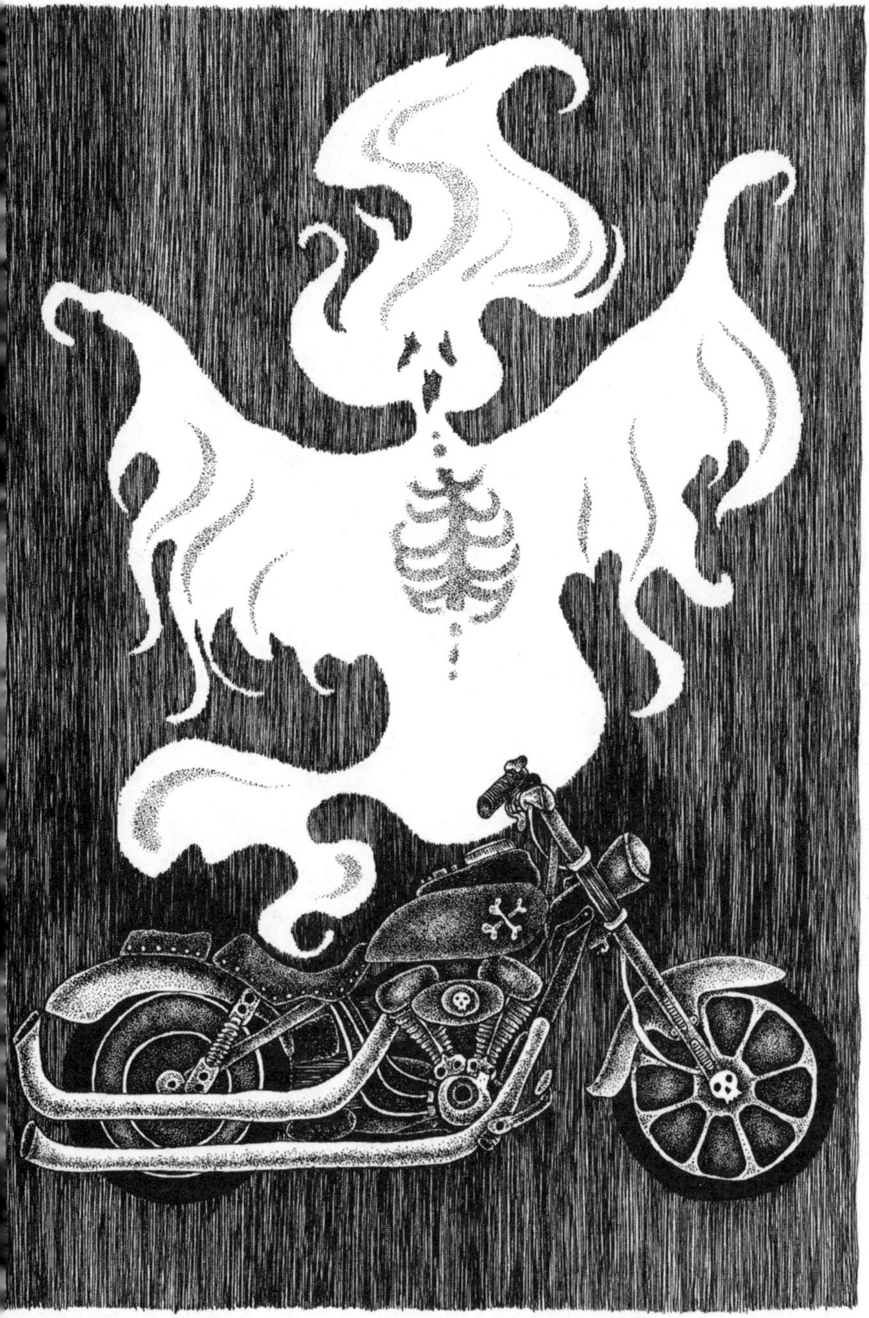

SNAKEBITE SUSAN

Snakebite Susan was a tough leathered bird
with a loud motorcycle that everyone heard
Susan would roar into town like a bomb
blaring her favorite old road-tripping songs

Susan once wrestled a bear to its knees
then ate fifty hot dogs with delicate ease
Susan once bet a King Cobra her eye
in a rowdy card game in the dead of the night

Her tattoos were roadmaps of where she had been
like the black leather vest she adorned with some pins
like her favorite motto, "Live to die, die to win"
and Susan did that all over again!

One lonely night on a cold desert road
black ice took her life when the bike lost control
twisted up like a pretzel, she climbed back on the steel
there rides Snakebite Susan, now a ghost at the wheel!

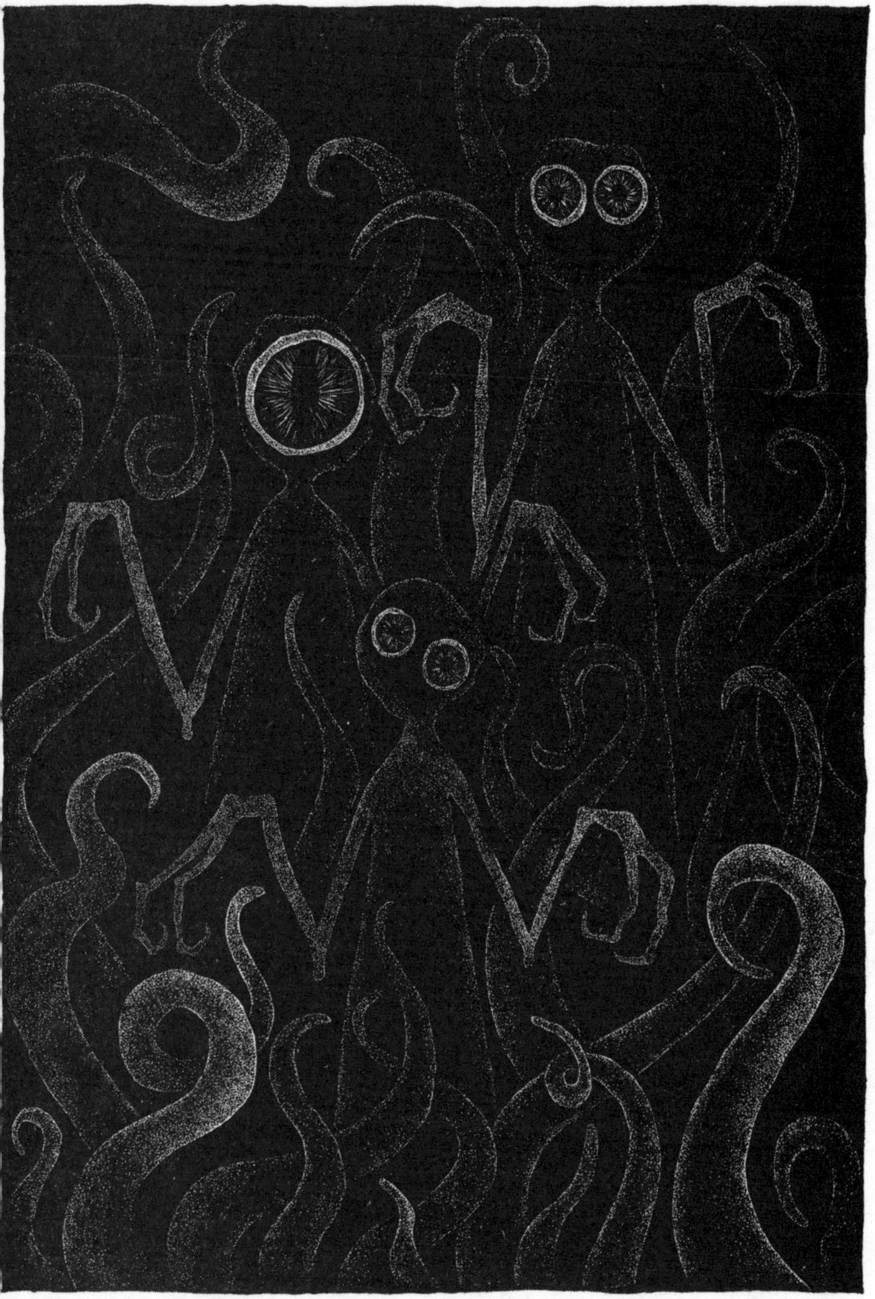

I DO!

Do you see them in the dead of night, I do…I do
Do they make you want to run in fright, like I do…I do
Do you think they know you're alone tonight?
'Cause I do…I do
What if they can see you now? Like I do…Boo!

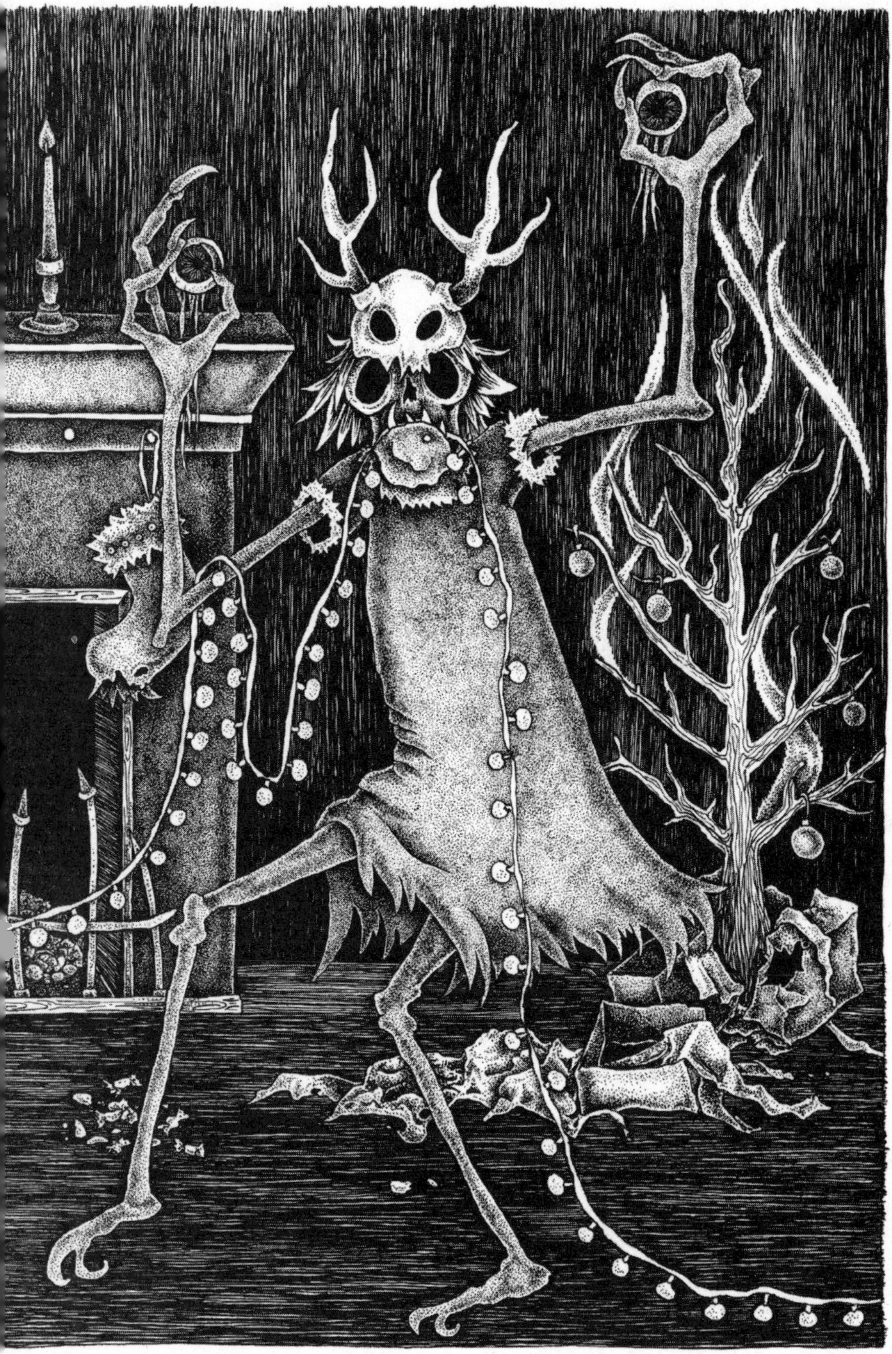

THE CHRISTMAS WITCH

She unwraps your presents while your family sleeps
She licks all of your cookies and sets fire to your tree
She ain't never going to like you, if you don't run,
she'll try to bite you
All she wants to do is spank you with a switch
Oh, ring that warning bell, it's the Christmas witch!

She makes a hissing sound when she tiptoes through your
house
But once you see her, it is too late to get out
Long nails to scratch your eyes out, she's gonna eat ya,
no doubt
This makes all your Christmas sweaters start to itch!
Oh, ring that warning bell, it's the Christmas witch

She stole the letter that you thought you mailed to Santa
"My name is Suzy Jones, and I really want a panda!"
In your neighborhood at night,
chewing on Christmas lights,
Somebody better go and flip that breaker switch
Oh, ring that warning bell, it's the Christmas witch!

She kicked your granny down the stairs at church
She slashes all your tires and leaves you in a lurch
She digs through your trash at night
She stole your brother's bike
She killed a reindeer, I just don't know which
Oh, ring that warning bell, it's the Christmas witch!

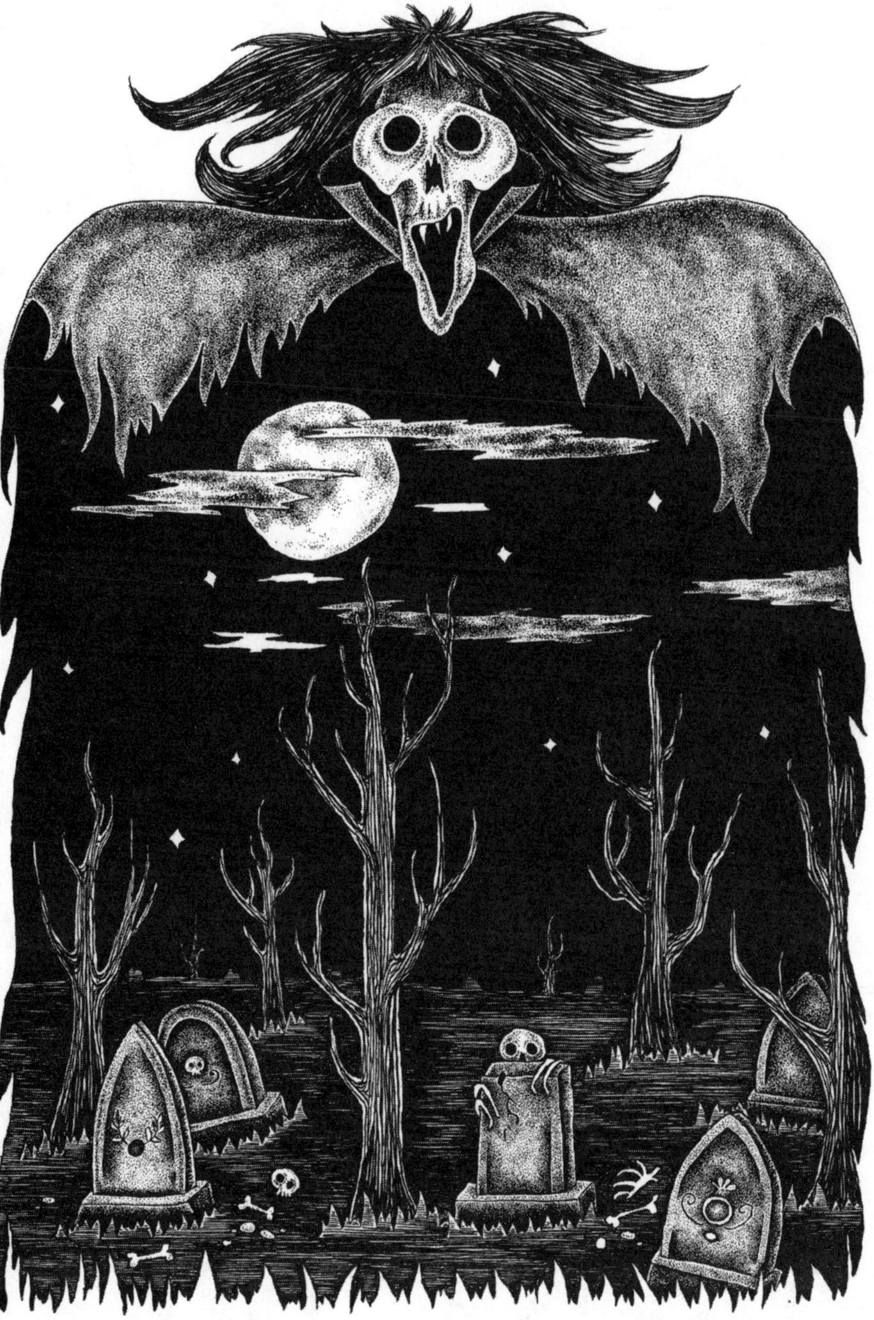

I AM THE NIGHT

I am the night, you may color me black
I lay still and quiet
like I'm not coming back
there is a corner of me
where you'll disappear
never to be seen
and never to hear
I am the night, you may color me death
where life can just vanish
in one single breath
there is a street where we hide
and wait in the dark
and without a sound
they tear you apart
for I am the night, you can call me the end
but if you see the sun rise
you will see me again

AFTERWORD

As a young Count, I had terrifying nightmares. Until about the age of ten, I was completely convinced that multiple monsters in the dark were out to get me. There were even some really scary ones that I wasn't expecting. For example, there is a poem in this book called "Mud on My Shoes." The morning after I had that nightmare, I walked into the kitchen to tell my mother, who was making me breakfast. Before I could say anything, she told me that a friend of the family had passed away last night, and it was the same woman in my dream! My mom didn't believe me at the time when I told her that I already knew, and that she had chased me down the hallway the night before. How can a ten-year-old make that up? I wonder if she believes me now.

Lucky for me—and maybe for you, too, if you survived this book and you're reading this far—I wrote them all down. Every last one of them, and all their horrible and slimy friends. I saved them all over the years like bad pennies in a jar. I figured even though they were kinda messed up, it didn't mean they were trash. They all have certainly found a use in my life. They taught me not to be afraid of things I didn't always understand. I also learned that not everything that looks scary might be scared of you too. Like spiders! How cool are they? What would you do with eight legs? You might have had a better chance in the muddy hallway with a dead lady chasing you. Then you are the scary one. I don't know any old ladies who like spiders, not even the dead ones.

In trying to learn how to conquer my fear of the darkness, I fell in love with creeps of all kinds.

If you're friends with them then you usually know where they are at night. Also, if they get to know you a little bit, they are less likely to want to bite on your toes while you sleep. Just make sure you tuck in the bottom of your sheet under your mattress, but I'll tell you about that later.

Creep Dreams!

xo,

Count D x

ACKNOWLEDGMENTS

This being the first complete published work of mine, the book itself was a labor of love that fell into incredibly supportive hands to which I could not be more grateful. I'd like to thank Tyson Cornell at Rare Bird for publishing these daydreams and night-screams. You are a brave night-light for love and art in this world that we all need. This book would not be possible without Rob "Blasko" Nicholson. Thank you for being a saint to human creeps and four-legged crawlers everywhere. Katrina Bleckley for keeping the nightmare alive and safe. My band and road family, Rob & Sheri Zombie, John 5, and Ginger for being my friends, and my ever inspiring real life Monster Squad. My spooky sister Ashley Costello who keeps Halloween Alive with me 365.

I would thank Wayne & Jackie Toth at Halloweentown for being the caretakers for those lost in the spooky universe. To my pal and amazingly talented illustrator Julia Yakovleva for being the queen of the creeps! Last but not least, to the goon behind the moon Justine Mette, you're a real party monster for sticking behind my madness. Thank you everyone from the bottom of my monster heart for making this book possible.

I'd like to dedicate this book to my parents, Robert and Kathy, my brother, Rusty, and my wife, Gabriela. I love you all so much, and thank for protecting me from the monsters. My furry children, Shaya, Norma, Ziggy, Rocky, Pee Wee, and Salem and Callie, for watching over me all through the night...the best nightmare watch ever! If it wasn't for all of my adopted animals I've had over the years, I might have lost some toes to those who lurk under the bed!

Count D. is an artist and musician known for his work with Rob Zombie and Alice Cooper. Originally from Texas, where he saw *Psycho* on television at the age of seven, and published his first poem ("There's a Monster in My Closet") at the age of nine, *All My Friends Are Creeps* is his first pub-lished collection of poetic works. He lives in Los Angeles with his family and five pets.

Julia Yakovleva was born in Russia. At the age of seven, her favorite film was *A Nightmare on Elm Street* and her favorite color was black. She now calls Cork, Ireland home, where she lives with her husband and daughter. Julia has a masters degree in design and a background in bookbinding.